BUSINESS MATH
EXCEL APPLICATIONS

Edward D. Laughbaum
The Ohio State University

Ken Seidel
Columbus State Community College

Upper Saddle River, New Jersey
Columbus, Ohio

Senior Acquisitions Editor: Gary Bauer
Editorial Assistant: Natasha Holden
Development Editor: Monica Ohlinger, Ohlinger Publishing Services
Production Editor: Louise N. Sette
Design Coordinator: Diane Ernsberger
Cover Designer: Bryan Huber
Production Manager: Pat Tonneman
Marketing Coordinator: Leigh Ann Sims

This book was printed and bound by OPM. The cover was printed by OPM.

Excel is a trademark of Microsoft.

Copyright © 2005 by Pearson Education, Inc., Upper Saddle River, New Jersey 07458.
Pearson Prentice Hall. All rights reserved. Printed in the United States of America. This publication is
protected by Copyright and permission should be obtained from the publisher prior to any prohibited
reproduction, storage in a retrieval system, or transmission in any form or by any means, electronic,
mechanical, photocopying, recording, or likewise. For information regarding permission(s), write to:
Rights and Permissions Department.

Pearson Prentice Hall™ is a trademark of Pearson Education, Inc.
Pearson® is a registered trademark of Pearson plc
Prentice Hall® is a registered trademark of Pearson Education, Inc.

Pearson Education Ltd.
Pearson Education Singapore Pte. Ltd.
Pearson Education Canada, Ltd.
Pearson Education—Japan

Pearson Education Australia Pty. Limited
Pearson Education North Asia Ltd.
Pearson Educación de Mexico, S.A. de C.V.
Pearson Education Malaysia Pte. Ltd.

10 9 8 7 6 5 4 3 2 1

ISBN 0-13-152682-0

PREFACE

Business Math Excel Applications contains applications from selected topics in an arithmetic-based business mathematics course. The intent of these materials is to introduce you to computers and to the software you will most likely use in college or on the job. Spreadsheet software is by far the most commonly used software in business. As a business mathematics student, you can expect to use spreadsheet software after you graduate. Using this project manual requires very little previous experience with computers or software. You will use a spreadsheet for the purpose of applying it to business mathematics. All of the text headings and business mathematics formulas are already in the projects; thus, you will not actually be "programming" as a businessperson might. When the business formulas are already in the spreadsheet worksheet, it is called a template. It is very common for businesspersons to use templates. If you want to learn more about spreadsheets, you can take a course like computer literacy or Excel.

It is expected that the material on any particular project will have been covered in class before it is assigned. There is an explanation of the formula-based mathematics used in each project; however, it is only a brief summary of the mathematics of that particular project and should not be considered a replacement for a standard business mathematics text or classroom instruction.

Before you sit at a computer to do a project, **please read the directions page** for the project to prepare you. When using the templates, read the entire screen to locate important information that is required to answer questions. Each project contains questions about the mathematics of the business application and questions about the related business topic. If you study the contents of individual cells in the spreadsheet, many times you will find mathematical formulas similar to those described on the mathematics page of each project. On several of the projects you may want to use a calculator for such things as finding how much data has changed between two altered worksheet templates, finding certain rates as requested, or altering the data.

As you do a project, it will be very helpful if you think of yourself as a businessperson. This may help you understand why each question is asked. That is, if you think of yourself as a student, you may only see the projects as a way to a grade for the course. The fact is that the questions asked are questions asked by businesspersons or consumers. They are questions that must be answered in the process of operating a business. Try to imagine why a businessperson wants to know the answers to the questions. Your goal is to understand the mathematics and the business of each project.

Acknowledgments

We would like to acknowledge the reviewers of this text: Bill Ferguson, Columbus State Community College; Jack Heinsius, Modesto Junior College; and Bunney Schmidt, Utah Valley State College.

CONTENTS

PROJECT 1
PAYROLL

Sample Computer Screens

Project 1: Payroll Templates

$\quad$ Hourly Wages

Enter your name in the box to the right $\qquad$ Name:

Payroll Record for the week ending December 17, 2003

Employee	Hourly Rate	Regular Hours	Overtime Hours	Regular Wages	Overtime Wages	Gross Wages	YTD Gross Wages
A. Einstein	$47.50	40	6	$1,900.00	$427.50	$2,327.50	$94,564.04
C. Sagan	$36.00	38	0	$1,368.00	$0.00	$1,368.00	$81,022.32
B. Franklin	$42.50	40	3	$1,700.00	$191.25	$1,891.25	$86,453.61
T. Paine	$42.50	25	0	$1,062.50	$0.00	$1,062.50	$86,851.64
L. Carroll	$27.75	40	0	$1,110.00	$0.00	$1,110.00	$55,735.25
A. Huxley	$38.25	40	3	$1,530.00	$172.13	$1,702.13	$75,888.11
Totals		223	12	$8,670.50	$790.88	$9,461.38	$480,514.97

Employee	FICA Tax	Medicare Tax	State Withholding	Federal Withholding	Local Tax Withholding	Net Wages
A. Einstein	$0.00	$33.75	$121.03	$470.30	$40.73	$1,702.42
C. Sagan	$84.82	$19.84	$71.14	$205.44	$23.94	$986.77
B. Franklin	$117.26	$27.42	$98.35	$346.72	$33.10	$1,301.50
T. Paine	$65.88	$15.41	$55.25	$124.04	$18.59	$801.92
L. Carroll	$68.82	$16.10	$57.72	$135.78	$19.43	$831.58
A. Huxley	$105.53	$24.68	$88.51	$295.66	$29.79	$1,187.74
Totals	$442.30	$137.19	$491.99	$1,577.95	$165.57	$6,811.94

Project 1: Payroll Templates

$\quad$ Piecework Wages

Enter your name in the box to the right $\qquad$ Name:

Amalgamated Widgets pays their widget twisters a fixed hourly wage based on experience plus a graduated piecerate wage as shown to the right.

Widgets Twisted	Piece rate per widget
0 to 100	$0.88
101 to 200	$1.12
201 to 350	$1.48
351 to 500	$1.96
501 or more	$2.33

Payroll Record for the week ending July 10, 2003

Employee	Hourly Rate	Hours Worked	Widgets Twisted	Hourly Wages	Piece rate Wages	Gross Wages
T. Edison	$3.25	47	472	$152.75	$661.12	$813.87
W. Wright	$3.35	65	530	$217.75	$785.90	$1,003.65
O. Wright	$4.00	40	318	$160.00	$374.64	$534.64
H. Ford	$2.35	32	164	$75.20	$159.68	$234.88
C. Klein	$3.00	25	210	$75.00	$214.80	$289.80
F. James	$5.32	18	180	$95.76	$177.60	$273.36
Totals		227	1874	$776.46	$2,373.74	$3,150.20

Project 1: Payroll Templates

Enter your name in the box to the right

Name:

High-Tech Electronics pays their sales associates an annual salary based on years of employment plus a graduated commission as shown to the right. Employees are paid monthly.	Monthly Sales		
	At Least	But Less Than	Commission
	$0	$5,000	0.0%
	$5,001	$8,000	3.0%
	$8,001	$12,000	5.0%
	$12,001	$18,000	8.0%
	$18,001		10.0%

Payroll Record for the month of May, 2003

Employee	Annual Salary	Monthly Salary	Monthly Sales	Commission	Gross Wages
G. Bush	$12,500	$1,041.67	$18,465	$816.50	$1,858.17
W. Clinton	$14,200	$1,183.33	$26,874	$1,657.40	$2,840.73
R. Reagan	$18,350	$1,529.17	$32,586	$2,228.60	$3,757.77
J. Carter	$18,500	$1,541.67	$16,450	$645.92	$2,187.59
G. Ford	$15,650	$1,304.17	$28,320	$1,802.00	$3,106.17
R. Nixon	$10,275	$856.25	$42,975	$4,316.75	$5,173.00
Totals	$89,475.00	$7,456.25	$165,670.00	$11,467.17	$18,923.42

DIRECTIONS:

1. Please read all directions. Study and analyze the computer screens before you start answering the questions. Most questions will require information from the computer screens.

2. Open Project 1 by selecting Project_01 on your hard drive or floppy disk (In Excel use File, Open). Set the *zoom* percentage for your screen resolution. For 640 by 480 pixels use a *zoom* setting of 55%, for a screen resolution of 800 by 600 pixels use a *zoom* setting of 75%, and for a screen resolution of 1024 by 768 pixels or higher use a *zoom* setting of 100%.

3. Project 1 contains three spreadsheets: an Hourly Wage spreadsheet, a Piecework Wages spreadsheet, and a Commission and Salary spreadsheet. Use the tabs on the bottom left of your screen to move between the different spreadsheets.

4. Only those cells in blue can be changed.

5. If you need to reset the data to the original values for Project 1—as in the sample screens above—simply **reopen the project** by clicking on the Excel commands File, Open and then select Project_01 followed by clicking on yes.

6. When you enter numeric data, do not include the $ or the , in the number. For example, to enter $35.00 you should enter 35 and to enter $1,765.56 you should enter 1765.56.

7. The Hourly Wage Spreadsheet assumes all employees will be paid an overtime rate equal to one and one half times their regular rate of pay for all hours in excess of 40 hours per week. The Piecework Wages spreadsheet assumes a straight hourly wage regardless of hours worked (no overtime).

7. To print a copy of the spreadsheet, select the print icon from the top toolbar.

8. To close this project and continue working in Excel, select the *close* option under the File menu. To exit Excel completely click on the **X** in the upper right corner of the screen. **Do not save your work.**

PROJECT 1 QUESTIONS

Hourly Wages Spreadsheet Questions

1. What are the total overtime wages and regular wages for all your employees if you give each of them 10 overtime hours for the week? Recall they must have 40 regular hours before they earn overtime.

2. What percent of total weekly gross is total weekly overtime pay if all your employees work 4 hours of overtime *per day* for 5 days?

3. Why is Einstein's FICA Tax $0.00?

4. If you have a rush job that requires 300 total hours to complete, what would be the total overtime cost to you if each employee worked the same number of hours? Print out a copy of this worksheet, circle the answer, and mark it as #4.

5. If the total 60 hours of overtime in Exercise 4 above is divided evenly among Sagan, Carroll, and Huxley, what will be your total weekly overtime cost for this job? Is this more or less than the overtime cost in Question 4?

6. Find an hourly rate for Franklin that causes his net wages to be as close to $1,500 as possible. What is this hourly rate?

7. Assuming a 40-hour week for all employees, if you give the first three employees a 12% hourly raise and the last three employees a 7% hourly raise, what will be the *increase* in your weekly gross wages? Don't forget to record on a paper notepad the current weekly gross before the raise.

8. Put your cursor in cell G10 and record the contents of the cell. Write this "Excel" formula as a typical "math" formula and record it on the answer sheet.

Piecework Wages Spreadsheet Questions

9. What are the weekly gross wages for Edison if he works 35 hours and twists 375 widgets?

10. Assume each employee worked 40 hours for the week and together they twisted 2,150 widgets. How many widgets should each employee twist if the total gross wages are as small as possible? Print this spreadsheet and mark it #10. Note: The total number of widgets twisted must be 2,150.

11. H. Ford wanted to earn some extra money so he worked a total of 72 hours and twisted 680 widgets. What are his gross wages and what is the percent increase in wages compared to a normal week in which he works 40 hours and twists 360 widgets?

12. What is the increase in total gross wages, compared to the original spreadsheet, if Amalgamated Widgets increases the piece rate per widget by 20%? *Note*: The original data is in the graphic at the beginning of this project.

Commission and Salary Spreadsheet Questions

13. Note the total gross wages. What is the percent increase in total gross wages if each salesperson has an additional $5,000 in sales?

14. What are Reagan's gross wages if he has $63,120 in total sales?

15. What must Ford's monthly sales be if his gross monthly wages are as close to $3,000 as possible?

16. Reset the original values for this spreadsheet. High-Tech is considering either option 1: a 5% increase in annual salaries; or option 2: adding 0.5% to each of its commission rates, excluding the 0% rate. Assume each salesperson's monthly sales stay the same. What are the gross monthly wages under each of these options? Which of these options has a lower total gross monthly wage?

PROJECT 1 ANSWERS

NAME_____   CLASS_____   HOUR_____

1.   Overtime wages_____   Regular wages_____

2.   _____

3.   _____

4.   Attach your printout with the problem marked #4 and the answer circled.

5.   _____

6.   _____

7.   _____

8.   _____   _____

9.   _____

10. Total gross wages_____   Attach a printout with the problem marked #10
                                                    and the answer circled.

11. Gross wages_____   Percent increase_____

12. Increase in total gross wages_____

13. Percent increase_____

14. Gross wages   _____

15. Monthly sales_____

16. Total gross wages option 1_____   option 2_____

     _____

MATHEMATICS USED IN PROJECT 1

HOURLY WAGES: Regular wages are based on the number of the regular hours worked. The hourly rate of pay should be thought of as the rate in the formula *Part = Base* times *Rate* ($P = B \cdot R$). Thus the formula becomes:

$$P = B \cdot R$$
$$RW = (RH) \cdot (HR)$$

where *RW*, *RH,* and *HR* represent regular wages, regular hours, and hourly rate respectively.

Overtime wages are paid at a rate of 1.5 times the regular hourly rate. Thus the wages earned for working overtime are based on the number of overtime hours worked. The formula $P = B \cdot R$ becomes:

$$P = B \cdot R$$
$$OW = 1.5 \cdot (OH) \cdot (HR)$$

where *OW*, *OH* and *HR* represent Overtime Wages, Overtime Hours and Hourly Rate, respectfully.

Gross wages are the sum of the regular wages and the overtime wages: $GW = RW + OW$.

After finding the gross wages, the net wages (net) are found by subtracting federal, state, and local withholding taxes as well as FICA and medicare taxes from the gross wages. The FICA tax rate is 6.2% of a worker's gross wages up to a maximum of $87,000 in annual wages. Thus employees with year-to-date gross wages in excess of $87,000 have either a reduced or $0 FICA withholding.
Using the formula

$$P = B \cdot R$$
$$FICA = 0.062 \cdot GW.$$

Medicare withholding is 1.45% of gross wages, thus from the formula

$$P = B \cdot R$$
$$Med = 0.0145 \cdot GW$$

In the calculation of federal withholding taxes, employees are assumed to be married with 2 withholding allowances. State withholding is assumed to be a flat 5.2% of gross wages and the local withholding is assumed to be a flat 1.75% of gross wages.

MATHEMATICS USED IN PROJECT 1

PIECEWORK WAGES: Hourly wages are calculated by multiplying the number of hours worked by the employee's hourly rate. In this piecework model the workers are not paid an overtime rate for weeks in which they work more than 40 hours. Generally, piecework employees are not paid an overtime rate since they earn more by completing more jobs, in this case, twisting widgets.

Piecework wages are calculated on a graduated scale. Workers are paid a fixed amount for each of the first 100 widgets they twist and then a greater amount for each of the widgets twisted between 101 and 200 and so forth.

Example: Determine the piece rate wages for a worker named Tom who has twisted 425 widgets.

Solution: Tom is paid $0.88 per widget for each of the first 100 widgets twisted. This leaves 325 widgets for which he must still be paid.

There are another 100 widgets in the 101 to 200 widget range and so Tom is paid $1.12 for each of these widgets. This leaves 225 widgets for which he must still be paid.

There are 150 widgets in the 201 to 350 widget range and since Tom still has to be paid for 225 completed widgets he is paid $1.48 for each of these. This leaves 75 widgets for which Tom must still be paid.

Tom is paid $1.96 for each of these final 75 widgets.
Tom's total piece rate wage then is $618.00:

$$100 \times \$0.88 = \$\ \ 88.00$$
$$100 \times \$1.12 = \$112.00$$
$$150 \times \$1.48 = \$222.00$$
$$\underline{75 \times \$1.96 = \$196.00}$$

then $88.00 + $112.00 + $222.00 + $196.00 = $618.00

Gross wages are calculated by adding hourly wages and piecework wages.

MATHEMATICS USED IN PROJECT 1

COMMISSION AND SALARY: Salespeople paid on a salary plus graduated commission scale earn a fixed salary for the pay period (the pay period is monthly for this project) and a percent of their total sales for the period. In this example the commission is set on a graduated scale that pays the salesperson a larger commission for a greater sales volume. A graduated commission scale is a motivational tool used to increase sales.

To calculate a salesperson's gross wages for the month, the payroll officer divides the salesperson's annual salary by 12 to determine their monthly salary. Then the salesperson's total sales for the month are recorded and the graduated commission scale is applied to determine their monthly commission. Gross wages are the sum of the salesperson's monthly salary and their total commission.

Example: Sarah is a salesperson with an annual salary of $12,000 and total monthly sales of $20,000. Calculate Sandy's gross wages for the month.

Solution: To calculate her gross wages for the month, we divide her annual salary by 12, $12,000 \div 12 = \$1,000$, to arrive at her monthly salary. Then we apply the commission scale to her sales figures.

There is no (0%) commission on the first $5,000 in sales, 3% commission on the next $3,000 in sales, 5% commission on the next $3,000, 8% commission on the next $6,000 in sales, and finally 10% commission on all monthly sales in excess of $18,000. Since Sarah had total sales of $20,000, her commission is calculated as follows:

Commission level	Sales at this level	Commission	Remaining sales eligible for commission
0%	$5,000	$0	$20,000 − $5,000 = $15,000
3%	$3,000	$.03 \times \$3,000 = \$90$	$15,000 − $3,000 = $12,000
5%	$3,000	$.05 \times \$3,000 = \$150$	$12,000 − $3,000 = $9,000
8%	$6,000	$.08 \times \$6,000 = \$480$	$9,000 − $6,000 = $3,000
10%	$3,000	$.10 \times \$3,000 = \$300$	$3,000 − $3,000 = $0

The total commission Sarah earned then is $90 + \$150 + \$480 + \$300 = \$1,020$.

Sarah's gross pay for the month is the sum of her monthly salary and her monthly commission is then $1,000 + \$1,020 = \$2,020$.

PROJECT 2
PAYROLL RECORD
Sample Computer Screen

Project 2: Paystub Template

Enter your name in the box to the right   Name: [   ]

Employee Information

Enter a 1 in the box beside the employee's marital status.

Married	1
Single	

Enter a 1 in the box beside the employee's payroll period.

Weekly	
Biweekly	
Semimonthly	
Monthly	1

Enter the State and Local income tax rates in the boxes below.

State Tax Rate	5.0%
Local Tax Rate	2.0%

Enter the number of withholding allowances in the box below.

Allowances	2

Enter the employee's gross pay in the box below.

Gross Pay	$8,146.65

Deductions:

Federal Withholding	$1,272.88
FICA:	$505.09
Medicare:	$118.13
State income tax:	$407.33
Local income tax:	$162.93
Medical Insurance:	$63.25
Dental Insurance:	$4.75
Life Insurance:	$8.50
Union Dues:	$25.00
401 K Plan:	$300.00
Other:	$0.00

Federal Withholding Tax Computations:

Withholding Allowance	$258.34
Income subject to withholding	$7,888.31
Amount to be withheld	$1,272.88

Gross Pay	$8,146.65

Total Deductions	$2,867.86

Net Pay	$5,278.79

DIRECTIONS:

1. Please read all directions. Study and analyze the computer screen before you start answering the questions. Most questions will require information from the computer screen.
2. Open Project 2 by selecting Project_02 on your hard drive or floppy disk (In Excel use File, Open). Set the *zoom* percentage for your screen resolution. For 640 by 480 pixels use a *zoom* setting of 55%, for a screen resolution of 800 by 600 pixels use a *zoom* setting of 75%, and for a screen resolution of 1024 by 768 pixels or higher use a *zoom* setting of 100%.
3. Project 2 contains two spreadsheets: a Payroll Record spreadsheet and Federal Withholding Tax (percent method) Computation spreadsheet. Only the Payroll Record spreadsheet will be used for this project. Use the tabs on the bottom left of your screen to move between the different spreadsheets.
4. Only cell values in blue can be changed.
5. When you enter numeric data, do not include the $ or the, in the number. For example, to enter $35.00 you should enter 35 and to enter $1,765.56 you should enter 1765.56.
6. If you need to reset the data to the original values for Project 2—as in the sample screens above—simply **reopen the project** by clicking on the Excel commands File, Open and then select Project_02 followed by clicking on yes.
7. To print a copy of the spreadsheet, select the print icon from the top toolbar.
8. To close this project and continue working in Excel, select the *close* option under the File menu. To exit Excel completely click on the X in the upper right corner of the screen. Do not save your work to disk.

PROJECT 2 QUESTIONS

If you have not already done so, reset the information using the sample screen at the beginning of this project.

1. For the data given on the screen, note the federal withholding tax and the net pay. Change the marital status of the employee from married to single. What is the increase in federal withholding tax? What is the decrease in net pay? Are these values the same?

2. A married person claiming 6 allowances is paid a monthly salary of $4,525.00. The state withholding tax rate is 5.75%, the local withholding tax rate is 1.5%, the individual pays $122.25 each month for medical insurance, $6.50 each month for dental insurance, deposits $250.00 in a 401k retirement plan, and does not have any other deductions. What is this person's monthly net pay and what are their total deductions?

3. Suppose the person in Question 2 above is given a 7% raise in their salary. All fixed deductions remain the same. What is the percent increase (decrease) in their net pay? Is it 7%? Why or why not?

4. Jon is a single person and is paid $2,800.00 biweekly. He claims 1 withholding allowance and is employed in a state with a withholding rate of 5%. The local withholding rate is 2%. Medical and dental insurance is paid by the company but Jon has life insurance premiums of $12 per pay period and union dues of $42.50 per pay period. He also contributes $25.00 each pay period to charity under *other* deductions. What are Jon's federal withholding tax deduction, total deductions, and net pay?

5. Suppose Jon from Question 4 above marries Kim who has two children. Change Jon's marital status from single to married and increase his withholding allowances from 1 to 4. What is the percent change in Jon's federal withholding tax and his net pay?

6. Reset the original values for this spreadsheet. What semimonthly gross pay must this person earn if their net pay needs to be as close as possible to $5,000?

7. A married person is paid a weekly salary of $835.00. What are the fewest number of federal withholding allowances they can claim if their federal withholding tax is $0?

8. Consider a single person, claiming one federal withholding allowance, with a biweekly salary of $8,650 who has no deductions other than federal withholding tax, FICA, Medicare, state withholding tax (5%), and local withholding tax (2%). Would this person's net pay increase more if they receive a 5% raise or if they get married? Don't forget to increase the number of withholding allowances to 2 if they get married.

9. For the single person described in Question 8 above, what percent increase in their biweekly salary would they have to earn to have their net pay be higher than it would have been had they married?

10. Marc is single and is paid a weekly salary of $625.00 and has no optional deductions. Lenny is single and paid a weekly salary of $6,250.00 and also has no optional deductions. Notice that Lenny is paid ten times as much as Marc. Is Lenny's net pay ten times as much as Marc's? Is it more or less than ten times?

11. For Marc and Lenny in Question 10 above, what percent of Marc's gross pay is his federal withholding tax? What percent of Lenny's gross pay is his federal withholding tax?

12. Frank is married and claims 4 withholding allowances and is paid a biweekly salary of $3,125.00. He has the option of having his $57.00 medical insurance premium deducted from his gross wages before his federal withholding tax is calculated. Investigate Frank's federal withholding tax savings by first listing the $57.00 as a medical insurance deduction and noting the federal withholding tax. Then list $0 as medical insurance deduction and increase Frank's gross pay by $57.00 and note the federal withholding tax. What is his biweekly withholding tax savings? What is his annual withholding tax savings?

PROJECT 2 ANSWERS

NAME_____   CLASS_____   HOUR_____

1.   Increase in federal withholding tax_____

       Decrease in net pay_____   Are these the same?_____

2.   Monthly net pay_____   Total deductions_____

3.   Percent increase in net pay_____

       Are these the same? Why or why not?_____

4.   Print out this spreadsheet and attach it to your answers.

5.   Percent change in federal withholding_____

       Percent change in net pay_____

6.   _____

7.   _____

8.   _____

9.   _____

10.   _____

11.   Marc's federal withholding tax is _____of his net pay.

       Lenny's federal withholding tax is _____of his net pay.

12.   Biweekly savings_____   Annual savings_____

11

MATHEMATICS USED IN PROJECT 2

The most complicated aspect of completing a payment record for an employee is the computation of federal withholding tax. In this template only the federal withholding tax requires the marital status, number of allowances claimed and the frequency of payments. Several states also use this information when calculating withholding but because of the wide variation in practice from state to state this template assumes a fixed percent is withheld for state income tax.

The computation of federal withholding tax requires three steps:

1. Calculate the withholding allowance by multiplying the number of allowances claimed by the value of an allowance. The value of an allowance depends on the frequency of payment. See the federal withholding spreadsheet for a table of withholding amounts.

    Example: A person paid semimonthly and claiming 3 allowances would have a withholding allowance of: $3 \times \$129.17 = \$387.51$, while a person paid weekly and claiming three allowances would have a withholding allowance of $3 \times \$59.62 = \$178.86$. Allowance values are from the federal withholding tax tables for wages paid through December, 2004.

2. Calculate the adjusted gross pay by subtracting the withholding allowance from the gross pay.

3. The federal withholding tax is computed on a progressive scale. That is, individuals with a higher income level have a greater percent of their income withheld. The withholding rate is also higher for single individuals than it is for married persons. The adjusted gross pay is used along with marital status and frequency of payments to identify the correct percentages to be applied to each individual. The Federal Withholding Tax Computations spreadsheet contains a copy of the percent method for federal withholding tables.

    Example: A single person with a weekly adjusted gross pay of $1,250.00 would have the following amounts withheld: (From Table 1a) 0% of the first $51, 10% of adjusted gross over $51 but not over $187, 15% of adjusted gross over $187 but not over $592, and finally 25% of all adjusted gross over $592. Thus the withholding would be:

$$0 \times 51 + 0.10 \times (187 - 51) + 0.15 \times (592 - 187) + 0.25 \times (1{,}250 - 592) = \$238.85$$

The withholding for a married individual with the same adjusted gross
pay, using Table 1b would be:

$$0 \times 154 + 0.10 \times (429 - 154) + 0.15 \times (1{,}245 - 429) + 0.25 \times (1{,}250 - 1{,}245) = \$151.15$$

FICA, Medicare, state withholding, and local withholding deductions are all found by computing a flat
percent of gross pay. The current FICA percent is 6.2% of gross pay up to a maximum of $87,000 in
annual gross wages. Medicare is 1.45% of gross pay. The state and local withholding rates depend on the
location of the place of employment. Other deductions such as insurance, union dues, retirement plans,
and savings plans are normally a fixed dollar amount per pay period. Total deductions are found by
summing all of the different deductions. Finally the net pay, or take-home pay, is found by subtracting
the total deductions from the gross pay.

PROJECT 3
SERIES TRADE DISCOUNTS

Sample Computer Screen

Project 3: Trade Discount Template

Enter your name in the box to the right   Name: [   ]

Item	Quantity	List Price Per Item	Total List Price Per Order	Discount 1	Discount 2	Discount 3	Net Price Per Item	Total Net Price Per Order	Single Discount Equivalent
SOFA	1	$750.00	$750.00	30	10	0	$472.50	$472.50	37.00%
EASY CHAIR	1	$565.00	$565.00	30	10	0	$355.95	$355.95	37.00%
STRAIGHT CHAIR	1	$385.00	$385.00	30	10	10	$218.30	$218.30	43.30%
TWIN BED	1	$280.00	$280.00	30	10	10	$158.76	$158.76	43.30%
FULL BED	1	$325.00	$325.00	30	20	5	$172.90	$172.90	46.80%
BRASS BED	1	$699.00	$699.00	30	20	5	$371.87	$371.87	46.80%
DRESSER	1	$450.00	$450.00	25	20	5	$256.50	$256.50	43.00%
MIRROR	1	$230.00	$230.00	25	20	5	$131.10	$131.10	43.00%
VANITY	1	$300.00	$300.00	50	20	5	$114.00	$114.00	62.00%
TABLE	1	$670.00	$670.00	50	20	0	$268.00	$268.00	60.00%
CHAIR	1	$200.00	$200.00	50	0	0	$100.00	$100.00	50.00%

Total Items   11   Total List $4,854.00   Total Net $2,619.87

Total Order Discount $2,234.13   Average Discount Rate for this Order   53.97%

DIRECTIONS:

1. Please read all directions. Study and analyze the computer screen before you start answering the questions. Most questions will require information from the computer screens.

2. Open Project 3 by selecting Project_03 on your hard drive or floppy disk (In Excel use File, Open). Set the *zoom* percentage for your screen resolution. For 640 by 480 pixels use a *zoom* setting of 55%, for a screen resolution of 800 by 600 pixels use a *zoom* setting of 75%, and for a screen resolution of 1024 by 768 pixels or higher use a *zoom* setting of 100%.

3. Project 3 contains one spreadsheet.

4. When you enter numeric data, do not include the $ or the , in the number. For example, to enter $35.00 you should enter 35 and to enter $1,765.56 you should enter 1765.56. Only cell values in blue can be changed.

5. If you need to reset the data to the original values for Project 3—as in the sample screens above— simply **reopen the project** by clicking on the Excel commands File, Open and then select Project_03 followed by clicking on yes.

6. To print a copy of the spreadsheet, select the print icon from the top toolbar.

7. To close this project and continue working in Excel, select the *close* option under the File menu. To exit Excel completely click on the X in the upper right corner of the screen. Do not save your work.

PROJECT 3 QUESTIONS

If you have not already done so, reset the information using the sample screen at the beginning of this project.

1. If discount 1 is 25% for all items, discount 2 is 25% for all items, and discount 3 is 0% for all items, what is the average discount rate?

2. If all items have discount rates of 10/10/5, what would the total discount and average discount rate be?

3. On all items that list for $500 and over, give trade discount rates of 20/10/5; on items that list for under $500, give trade discount rates of 10/10/5. What is the total discount and average discount rate?

4. Leave all of the discount rates the same as they were for Question 3 above and change the quantity ordered to 5 of each item. What is the change in the total discount and the average discount rate? Explain your answers.

5. For an order of only 1 sofa and nothing else, find the net price, the single discount equivalent, and the average discount rate if the trade discounts are 40/0/0; 40/10/0; 40/20/10; and 40/30/20.

6. You need to restock your store and must order 5 sofas, 8 easy chairs, 12 straight chairs, 4 twin beds, 2 full beds, 1 brass bed, 5 dressers, 4 mirrors, 0 vanities, 1 table and 6 chairs. Because of the size of your order the manufacturer offers you trade discounts of 30/20/10 on any item you are ordering 4 or more of and 20/10/10 on all other items. What is the total net price of your order?

7. Reset the order quantities to 1 for each item. Adjust the trade discount rates in any way you choose so that the total discount is approximately $2,500.00. Print out a copy of this spreadsheet.

8. Reset the original values from the sample screen at the beginning of this project and note the total net price. If you add $50 to the list price of each item, what is the increase in the total net price?

9. Reset the original values from the sample screen at the beginning of this project and note the total net price. Increase the list price of each item by 15% and note the amount of the increase in the total net price. Does the total net selling price increase by 15%? Does the average discount rate increase by 15%?

10. In Question 9, what formula or formulas did you use to find the new list price after the 15% increase?

11. Give the easy chair and the straight chair a series trade discount of 10/10/5 and find the single discount equivalent for each of these items. Are the single discount equivalents the same? Change the order to 10 easy chairs. Is the single discount equivalent still the same? Explain.

12. If you were working Question 5 without the computer, what formula would you use to calculate the net price of the sofa?

13. Does the series trade discount 30/20/10 yield the same net price as the series trade discount 10/20/30? Why or why not?

14. You have $10,000 available to buy stock for your store. The manufacturer will give a 30/20/10 series trade discount for orders of 5 or more items and 20/10/5 for orders of 4 or fewer items. Select as many of each item, adjusting the trade discounts as necessary, to stock your store. Spend as much of your $10,000 as possible without going over budget. Print out this spreadsheet and attach it to your answers.

15. Put your cursor in cell K10 and record the contents of the cell. Write this "Excel" formula as a typical "math" formula and record it on the answer sheet.

PROJECT 3 ANSWERS

NAME_____ CLASS_____ HOUR_____

1. Average rate_____

2. Total discount_____   Average rate_____

3. Total discount_____   Average rate_____

4. Change in total discount_____   Change in average rate_____

   Explain_____

5. 40/0/0 Net_____   40/0/0 SDE_____   40/0/0 Average_____

   40/10/0 Net_____   40/10/0 SDE_____   40/10/0 Average_____

   40/20/10 Net_____   40/20/10 SDE_____   40/20/10 Average_____

   40/30/20 Net_____   40/30/20 SDE_____   40/30/20 Average_____

6. Total net price_____

7. On the printout, circle the $2,500 and mark the answer as #7.

8. Increase in total net price_____

9. _____

10. _____

11. Same?_____   Same?_____   Explain_____

12. _____

13. _____ Yes   No

14. Circle the printout answer and mark it #14.

15. _____   _____

MATHEMATICS USED IN PROJECT 3

Trade discounts, and in particular, series trade discounts, are sequentially applied percent problems. In these situations it is important to realize that the net price is the difference between the list price and discount. $Net = List - Discount$. The list price is generally a known amount as is the discount rate. To calculate the discount for a single trade discount problem we use the basic percent equation, $Part = Base \times Rate$ with the discount rate as the *Rate*, the list price as the *Base*, and the discount as the *Part*. $Discount = List\ Price \times Discount\ Rate$.

It is important to notice that problems such as these can also be solved using complementary rates. If an item is offered with a 20% discount rate this means that the net price must be 80% of the list price. $Net = Complementary\ Rate \times List\ Price$. 20% and 80% are complementary rates because their sum is 100%. Any time we are looking at a percent discount we can just as easily consider using complements. Complementary percent rates are found by subtracting the discount rate from 100%.

> **Example**: What is the net price of an item offered with a list price of $60.00 and a 30% trade discount?
>
> **Solution I:** Using the discount rate:
>
> We calculate the discount: $Discount = List\ Price \times Discount\ Rate$, $Discount = \$60.00 \times 0.30 = \$18.00$. Then we can calculate the net price: $Net = List - Discount$, and so $Net = \$60.00 - \$18.00 = \$42.00$.
>
> **Solution II:** Using complementary rates:
>
> The complement of a 30% discount rate would be $100\% - 30\% = 70\%$, then $Net\ Price = Complementary\ Rate \times List\ Price$.
>
> So $Net\ Price = 0.70 \times \$60.00 = \$42.00$.
>
> If we wanted to find the actual discount received we could subtract the net price from the list price. $Discount = \$60.00 - \$42.00 = \$18.00$.

When we are considering a series trade discount, the use of complementary percent rates is almost invaluable. Consider a 30/20/10 series trade discount. This means the first member in the distribution chain receives a discount of 30% off the list price. The next member of the distribution chain receives a discount of 20% off of the first member's price and finally the third member of the chain receives a discount of 10% of the second member's price. This last price is what we call the net price of the item. When this is expressed using the complementary rates of 70%, 80%, and 90% we can see that the first member of the chain pays 70% of the list price, the second member pays 80% of the first member's price or 80% of 70% of list price and that the net price is 90% of the second member's price or 90% of 80% of 70% of the list price. While this sounds rather confusing it is readily translated into mathematics using the basic percent equation idea that the word "of" means we should multiply. $Net\ Price = 0.90 \times 0.80 \times 0.70 \times List\ Price$

Example: What is the net price of an item offered with a list price of $60.00 and a 20/10/5 series trade discount?

Solution I: Using the discount rate:

We calculate the first discount: $Discount = List\ Price \times Discount\ Rate$, $Discount = \$60.00 \times 0.20 = \$12.00$ then we can calculate the first member's price: $Price1 = \$60.00 - \$12.00 = \$48.00$. Then we calculate the second member's discount: $Discount = \$48.00 \times 0.10 = \$4.80$ and their price: $Price2 = \$48.00 - \$4.80 = \$43.20$. Finally we calculate the final member's discount: $Discount = \$43.20 \times 0.05 = \$2.16$ and the net price: $Net\ Price = \$43.20 - \$2.16 = \$41.04$

Solution II: Using complementary rates:

The complementary rates for a 20/10/5 series trade discount would be 80%, 90%, and 95%. Then we can calculate the net price using $Net\ Price = Product\ of\ Complementary\ Rate \times List\ Price$.

So $Net\ Price = 0.80 \times 0.90 \times 0.95 \times \$60.00 = \$41.04$.

If we wanted to find the actual discount received we could subtract the net price from the list price. $Discount = \$60.00 - \$41.04 = \$18.96$.

The single discount equivalent of a series trade discount is the single discount rate, which would result in the same net price as the series trade discount. It is important to note that the single discount equivalent is not the sum of the discount rates. We calculate the single discount equivalent (SDE) be finding the complement of the product of the complements of the discount rates.

$SDE = 100\% - (100\% - Rate1) \times (100\% - Rate2) \times (100\% - Rate3)$.

Example: Find the single discount equivalent of a 30/20/10 series trade discount

Solution: The complements of the rates are 70%, 80%, and 90% and $0.70 \times 0.80 \times 0.90 = .504 = 50.4\%$, so $SDE = 100\% - 50.4\% = 49.6\%$.

PROJECT 4
MARKUP

Sample Computer Screens

Project 4: Markup Template

MARKUP BASED ON COST

Enter your name in the box to the right

Name: [   ]

Item	Cost	Markup Rate Based on Cost	Markup Rate Based on Selling Price	Markup	Selling Price
Computer	$1,200.00	30.0%	23.1%	$360.00	$1,560.00
Monitor	$625.00	35.0%	25.9%	$218.75	$843.75
CD-ROM	$88.00	50.0%	33.3%	$44.00	$132.00
DVD Drive	$535.00	60.0%	37.5%	$321.00	$856.00
Printer	$250.00	40.0%	28.6%	$100.00	$350.00
Totals	$2,698.00			$1,043.75	$3,741.75

Average Markup Rate based on Cost =	38.69%

Project 4: Markup Template

MARKUP BASED ON SELLING PRICE

Enter your name in the box to the right

Name: [   ]

Item	Cost	Markup Rate Based on Cost	Markup Rate Based on Selling Price	Markup	Selling Price
Television	$1,625.00	25.0%	20.0%	$406.25	$2,031.25
DVD Player	$350.00	33.3%	25.0%	$116.67	$466.67
VCR	$110.00	42.9%	30.0%	$47.14	$157.14
Reciever & Speakers	$525.00	150.0%	60.0%	$787.50	$1,312.50
Sub Woofer	$130.00	66.7%	40.0%	$86.67	$216.67
Totals	$2,740.00			$1,444.23	$4,184.23

Average Markup Rate based on Selling Price =	34.52%

DIRECTIONS:

1. Please read all directions. Study and analyze the computer screens before you start answering the questions. Most questions will require information from the computer screens.

2. Open Project 4 by selecting Project_04 on your hard drive or floppy disk (In Excel use File, Open). Set the *zoom* percentage for your screen resolution. For 640 by 480 pixels use a *zoom* setting of 55%, for a screen resolution of 800 by 600 pixels use a *zoom* setting of 75%, and for a screen resolution of 1024 by 768 pixels or higher use a *zoom* setting of 100%.

3. Project 4 contains 2 spreadsheets, Markup Based on Cost and Markup Based on Selling Price. **Use the file tabs in the lower left corner of the worksheet to move between spreadsheets.**

4. When you enter numeric data, do not include the $ or the , in the number. For example, to enter $1,765.56 you should enter 1765.56. To enter a percentage you must enter the value in decimal form. To enter a markup rate of 30% you must type .30. Only cell values in blue can be changed.

5. If you need to reset the data to the original values for Project 4—as in the sample screens above—simply **reopen the project** by clicking on the Excel commands File, Open and then select Project_04 followed by clicking on yes.

6. To print a copy of the spreadsheet, select the print icon from the top toolbar.

PROJECT 4 QUESTIONS

If you have not already done so, reset the information using the sample screens at the beginning of this project.

1. On the Markup Based on Cost spreadsheet, adjust the markup rate based on cost so that the total markup is as near to $4,000.00 as you can make it. Print out a copy of this worksheet. Circle the total markup and mark the page as #1.

2. On the Markup Based on Selling Price spreadsheet, adjust the markup rate based on selling price so that the total markup is as near to $4,000.00 as you can make it. Print out a copy of this worksheet. Circle the total markup and mark the page as #2.

3. On the Markup Based on Cost spreadsheet, adjust all the markup rates so that the average markup rate is approximately 200% (do not make all rates 200%). Print out a copy of this worksheet. Circle the average markup rate and mark it as #3.

4. On the Markup Based on Selling Price spreadsheet, adjust all the markup rates so that the average rate is approximately 80% (do not make all rates 80%). Print out a copy of this worksheet. Circle the average markup rate and mark it as #4.

5. On the Markup Based on Cost spreadsheet, what would be the total markup if all items had a markup rate based on cost of 125% (give all 5 items a 125% markup rate). Answer the same question for 100%, 150%, and 300%.

6. On the Markup Based on Selling Price spreadsheet, what is the selling price of the VCR if the markup rate is 50%, 70%, 90%, 95%, and 100%? What happens when the markup rate is 100%? Explain why you think this happens.

7. Reload the original Project 4 template or reset the original values from the sample screens (to get back the original data) and write in your notes the **total** price, **total** cost, and **total** markup on the Markup Based on Cost spreadsheet. Increase the cost of each item by 10%. What is the dollar amount of the increase in total selling price, total cost, and total markup? Are these all 10% increases as well?

8. Reload the original Project 4 template or reset the original values from the sample screens (to get back the original data). On the Markup Based on Selling Price spreadsheet, add $40 to the cost of each item. What is the increase in the total selling price, total cost and total markup?

9. The formula for markup based on cost is $M = C \times R_c$. Move the cursor arrow to cell F10 and copy the formula from the template onto the answer sheet. In the mathematical formula $M = C \times R_c$, C represents the cost and R_c represents the rate based on cost. In the formula from the template, what do C10 and D10 represent?

10. Using mathematics (without the help of the spreadsheet), convert a 400% markup rate based on the cost to an equivalent rate based on selling price.

11. Using mathematics (without the help of the spreadsheet), convert an 80% markup rate based on the selling price to an equivalent rate based on cost.

12. On the Markup Based on Cost spreadsheet, put your cursor in cell E8 and record the contents of the cell. Write this "Excel" formula as a typical "math" formula and record it on the answer sheet.

PROJECT 4 ANSWERS

NAME_____ CLASS_____ HOUR_____

1. On the printout, circle the total markup and mark the page as #1.

2. On the printout, circle the total markup and mark the page as #2.

3. On the printout, circle the total markup and mark the page as #3.

4. On the printout, circle the total markup and mark the page as #4.

5. 125% Markup rate   Total markup_____

    100% Markup rate   Total markup_____

    150% Markup rate   Total markup_____

    300% Markup rate   Total markup_____

6. 50% Markup rate   Selling price_____

    70% Markup rate   Selling price_____

    90% Markup rate   Selling price_____

    95% Markup rate   Selling price_____

    100% Markup rate   Selling price_____

    Explain_____

7. Increase in total selling price_____   Increase in total cost_____

    Increase in total markup_____   Explain_____

8. Increase in total selling price_____   Increase in total cost_____

    Increase in total markup_____   Explain_____

9. _____

10. _____

11. _____

12. _____   _____

MATHEMATICS USED IN PROJECT 4

If the markup M is based on the cost price C, this means that from the formula $P = B \times R$, the base number is C and the M is the part number. Since markup can be based on cost or selling price (see below), the markup rate based on cost will be symbolized as R_c. The markup formula comes from $P = B \times R$.

$$\text{from} \qquad P = B \times R$$
$$M = C \times R_c$$

Experience suggests that the selling price can be found by adding the markup M to the cost C. That is:

$S = C + M$	Now, since $M = C \times R_c$ replace M with $C \times R_c$
$S = C + C \times R_c$	and since $C = 1 \times C$, replace C with $1 \times C$
$S = 1 \times C + C \times R_c$	now factor the C to the front
$S = C(1 + R_c)$.	

Thus you can find the selling price when the cost and the markup rate are known. Multiply the cost by the sum of 1 plus the markup rate.

If the markup M is based on the selling price, the base number in the formula $P = B \times R$ becomes the selling price S. The markup rate is described by R_s, indicating that the rate is based on selling price. The formula $P = B \times R$ becomes:

$$\text{from} \qquad P = B \times R$$
$$M = S \times R_s$$

As was done above, the selling price can be found by adding markup to cost.

Another method for finding the selling (sales) price is shown below where M is replaced with $S \times R_s$ in the formula $S = C + M$.

$S = C + M$	replace M with $S \times R_s$
$S = C + S \times R_s$	subtract $S \times R_s$ from both sides of the equation
$S - S \times R_s = C$	replace S with $1 \times S$
$1 \times S - S \times R_s = C$	factor the S to the front
$S(1 - R_s) = C$	and finally, divide both sides of the equation by $(1 - R_s)$
$S = \dfrac{C}{(1 - R_s)}$	

PROJECT 5
SIMPLE INTEREST AND SIMPLE DISCOUNT

Sample Computer Screens

Project 5: Simple Interest, Simple Discount Template

Simple Interest

Enter your name in the box to the right   Name: [   ]

Principal	Annual Rate	Days	Exact Interest	Exact Maturity Value		Ordinary Interest	Ordinary Maturity Value
$100.00	2.0%	300	$1.64	$101.64		$1.67	$101.67
$1,000.00	3.0%	250	$20.55	$1,020.55		$20.83	$1,020.83
$10,000.00	4.0%	30	$32.88	$10,032.88		$33.33	$10,033.33
$100,000.00	5.0%	10	$136.99	$100,136.99		$138.89	$100,138.89
Totals $111,100.00			$192.05	$111,292.05		$194.72	$111,294.72

Principal	Annual Rate	Months	Interest	Maturity Value
$100.00	2.0%	12	$2.00	$102.00
$1,000.00	3.0%	12	$30.00	$1,030.00
$10,000.00	4.5%	6	$225.00	$10,225.00
$100,000.00	1.5%	3	$375.00	$100,375.00
Totals $111,100.00			$632.00	$111,732.00

Project 5: Simple Interest, Simple Discount Template

Simple Discount

Enter your name in the box to the right   Name: [   ]

Face Value	Discount Rate	Days	Exact Discount	Exact Proceeds		Ordinary Discount	Ordinary Proceeds
$100.00	2.0%	300	$1.64	$98.36		$1.67	$98.33
$1,000.00	3.0%	250	$20.55	$979.45		$20.83	$979.17
$10,000.00	6.0%	30	$49.32	$9,950.68		$50.00	$9,950.00
$100,000.00	5.0%	10	$136.99	$99,863.01		$138.89	$99,861.11
Totals $111,100.00			$208.49	$110,891.51		$211.39	$110,888.61

Face Value	Discount Rate	Months	Discount	Proceeds
$100.00	2.0%	12	$2.00	$98.00
$1,000.00	3.0%	12	$30.00	$970.00
$10,000.00	4.5%	6	$225.00	$9,775.00
$100,000.00	1.5%	3	$375.00	$99,625.00
Totals $111,100.00			$632.00	$110,468.00

25

Project 5: Simple Interest, Simple Discount Template

Enter your name in the box to the right   Name: [   ]

				Place a 1 below the cell representing the units of time being used.						
Principal	Rate	Time	Exact Days	Ordinary Days	Months	Years	Time Units per Year	Unknown Interest	Unknown Maturity Value
$1,000.00	5.0%	90		1			360	$12.50	$1,012.50
Principal	Unknown Rate	Time	Exact Days	Ordinary Days	Months	Years	Time Units per Year	Interest	Maturity Value
$1,000.00	5.0%	90		1			360	$12.50	$1,012.50
Principal	Rate	Unknown Time	Exact Days	Ordinary Days	Months	Years	Time Units per Year	Interest	Maturity Value
$1,000.00	5.0%	90		1			360	$12.50	$1,012.50
Unknown Principal	Rate	Time	Exact Days	Ordinary Days	Months	Years	Time Units per Year	Interest	Maturity Value
$1,000.00	5.0%	90		1			360	$12.50	$1,012.50

DIRECTIONS:

1. Please read all directions. Study and analyze the computer screens before you start answering the questions. Most questions will require information from the computer screens.

2. Open Project 5 by selecting Project_05 on your hard drive or floppy disk (In Excel use File, Open). Set the *zoom* percentage for your screen resolution. For 640 by 480 pixels use a *zoom* setting of 55%, for a screen resolution of 800 by 600 pixels use a *zoom* setting of 75%, and for a screen resolution of 1024 by 768 pixels or higher use a *zoom* setting of 100%.

3. Project 5 contains four spreadsheets, Simple Interest, Simple Discount, Finding Unknowns, and a days-of-the-year table. Use the tabs in the lower left corner of the worksheet to move between spreadsheets.

4. When you enter numeric data, do not include the $ or the , in the number. For example, to enter $1,765.56 you should enter 1765.56. To enter a percentage you must enter the value in decimal form. To enter 30% you must type .30. Only cell values in blue can be changed.

5. If you need to reset the data to the original values for Project 5—as in the sample screens above—simply **reopen the project** by clicking on the Excel commands File, Open and then select Project_05 followed by clicking on yes.

6. To print a copy of the spreadsheet, select the print icon from the top toolbar.

7. To close this project and continue working in Excel, select the *close* option under the File menu. To exit Excel completely click on the X in the upper right corner of the screen. Do not save your work to disk.

PROJECT 5 QUESTIONS

If you have not already done so, reset the information using the sample screens at the beginning of this project.

Simple Interest Questions

1. Find the **exact** interest earned from each investment of the following: $4,000 at 12% for 90 days, $6,000 at 10% for 180 days, $5,000 at 11% for 365 days, and $10,000 at 13% for 270 days.

2. Find the **ordinary** interest on the investments in Question 1.

3. Find the **exact** and **ordinary** maturity values of $10,000 invested at 12% for 30, 60, 90, and 400 days. Put all of this information on the same screen and print this page.

4. What is the difference in interest earned between an investment of $40,000 at 14% ordinary interest for 60 days and an investment of $40,000 at 14% interest for 2 months? Explain.

5. Would it be better to invest $50,000 at 12% exact interest for 240 days or $50,000 at 11.85% ordinary interest for 240 days? Would you change your mind if this were a simple interest loan?

6. Approximately how much time (in days) is required for an investment of $10,000 at 12% exact interest to grow to $12,500?

7. Use the Days-of-the-Year spreadsheet to determine the duration of a $15,000 exact simple interest loan signed on May 19, 2003 and due on September 7, 2003. What is the maturity value of this loan if the interest rate is 16%?

8. Put your cursor in cell E7 and record the contents of the cell. Write this "Excel" formula as a typical "math" formula and record it on the answer sheet.

Simple Discount Questions

9. What is the **exact** discount for each of the following simple discount loans: $4,000 at 12% for 90 days, $6,000 at 10% for 180 days, $5,000 at 11% for 365 days, and $10,000 at 13% for 270 days.

10. Use this spreadsheet to determine what the face value of an 8% simple discount note due in 18 months must be if the proceeds must be as close to $20,000 as possible?

11. What must be the face value of a 12% ordinary simple discount note due in 200 days if the proceeds of the note must be $40,000? What is the discount on this note?

12. In Question 9 above, would the borrower save money by borrowing $40,000 at 12% ordinary simple interest due in 200 days? Why?

13. Use the days of the year spreadsheet to help find the discount and proceeds on a 7% simple discount note with a face value of $16,000 if the note was signed on October 23, 2002 and was due on June 7, 2003.

Finding Unknowns

14. How much must be invested at 9% ordinary simple interest to earn $800 interest in 10, 100, 200, and 500 days?

15. How long (in days) will it take an investment of $1,000 at 9% exact simple interest to earn $200 in interest?

16. If an investment of $8,000 earned $840 in interest in 7 months, what was the simple interest rate?

17. How much would you need to invest today at 11% simple interest in order to earn $6,000 in interest in 7 years?

PROJECT 5 ANSWERS

NAME_____   CLASS_____   HOUR_____

1. $4,000 investment_____ $6,000 investment_____

      $5,000 investment_____ $10,000 investment_____

2. $4,000 investment_____ $6,000 investment_____

      $5,000 investment_____ $10,000 investment_____

3.   Attach the printout with the answer circled and marked as #3.

4.   _____

      _____

5.   _____

      _____

6.   _____

7.   Loan duration_____days   Maturity value_____

8.   _____   _____

9. $4,000 Loan_____ $6,000 Loan_____

      $5,000 Loan_____ $10,000 Loan_____

10.   Face value_____

11.   Face value_____   Discount_____

12.   _____

13.   Discount_____   Proceeds_____

14.   10 days_____   100 days_____

      200 days_____   500 days_____

15.   _____days

16.   Rate_____

17.   Investment_____

28

MATHEMATICS USED IN PROJECT 5

Money that is either invested or borrowed is called principal. You usually earn money, called interest, on what you have invested or pay a lender interest on money you have borrowed. That is, the interest you earn or pay is based on the principal invested or borrowed. Businesses quite often deal in simple interest investments and simple interest loans. A simple interest investment (or loan) earns interest according to the basic percent formula $P = B \times R$ or Part equals Base times Rate. We can use the basic percent equation as model for our simple interest formula and merely change the names of the variables to reflect our work with finance. Rather than Part, (P), we are interested in Interest, (I). Instead of Base, (B), we have Principal, (P), and we replace the Rate (R) with the product of the annual interest rate (R) and the investment/loan's duration or time (T). The reason we must use the product of the interest rate and time is because the interest rate is always stated as a percent per year. If our investment or loan is of a duration less than 1 year then the interest rate must be adjusted to reflect that. For example if an investment with a duration of 1 year would earn \$100 in simple interest, then an investment with an equal principal and interest rate but a duration of only 6 months should only earn half as much interest.

The Simple Interest Formula then is $I = P \times R \times T$, where T represents time in years.

The maturity value, (M), is the sum of the principal and interest, $M = P + I$.

The maturity value can also be found with another formula show below.

Since	$M = P + I$ and $I = P \times R \times T$
then	$M = P + P \times R \times T$
and finally	$M = P(1 + R \times T)$

For a loan or investment with a duration given in days, this template uses two kinds of simple interest. The first kind is exact interest. As the name implies, exact interest uses the exact time in a calculation. This means that when time is in days it is converted to years by dividing by 365. The other simple interest form used in this worksheet is ordinary interest. Ordinary interest implies a 360 day year and so we convert days to years by dividing by 360. The ordinary year is a leftover from the days before calculators and computers. It is much easier to divide by 360 than by 365 when we are working with only pencil and paper.

PROJECT 6
COMPOUND INTEREST

Sample Computer Screen

Project 6: Compound Interest Template

Enter your name in the box to the right   Name:[   ]

Future Value Compound Interest

Principal	Annual Rate	Time (In Years)	Periods Per Year	Total Account Balance	Interest Earned
$10,000.00	12.0%	5	4	$18,061.11	$8,061.11
$10,000.00	12.0%	10	4	$32,620.38	$22,620.38
$10,000.00	12.0%	20	4	$106,408.91	$96,408.91
$10,000.00	12.0%	50	4	$3,693,558.15	$3,683,558.15
$10,000.00	12.0%	75	4	$70,985,134.83	$70,975,134.83

$50,000.00		Totals		$74,835,783.37	$74,785,783.37

Present Value Compound Interest

Amount Needed	Annual Rate	Time (In Years)	Periods Per Year	Principal Required
$25,000.00	8.0%	5	12	$16,780.26

DIRECTIONS:

1. Please read all directions. Study and analyze the computer screen before you start answering the questions. Most questions will require information from the computer screen.

2. Open Project 6 by selecting Project_06 on your hard drive or floppy disk (In Excel use File, Open). Set the *zoom* percentage for your screen resolution. For 640 by 480 pixels use a *zoom* setting of 55%, for a screen resolution of 800 by 600 pixels use a *zoom* setting of 75%, and for a screen resolution of 1024 by 768 pixels or higher use a *zoom* setting of 100%.

3. Project 6 contains one spreadsheet, Compound Interest.

4. When you enter numeric data, do not include the $ or the , in the number. For example, to enter $1,765.56 you should enter 1765.56. To enter a percentage you must enter the value in decimal form. To enter 30% you must type .30. Only cell values in blue can be changed.

5. If you need to reset the data to the original values for Project 6—as in the sample screens above—simply **reopen the project** by clicking on the Excel commands File, Open and then select Project_06 followed by clicking on yes.

6. To print a copy of the spreadsheet, select the print icon from the top toolbar.

7. To close this project and continue working in Excel, select the *close* option under the File menu. To exit Excel completely click on the X in the upper right corner of the screen. Do not save your work to disk.

PROJECT 6 QUESTIONS

If you have not already done so, reset the information using the sample screens at the beginning of this project.

1. Find the interest earned on an investment of $12,000 at 10% for 10 years compounded annually, semiannually, quarterly, monthly, and daily.

2. If you invest $4,000 at 8% compounded quarterly for 3 years, $6,000 at 9.2% compounded semiannually for 4 years, $10,000 at 11.1% compounded quarterly for 2 years, and $3,000 at 13.5% compounded monthly for 7 years, how much total interest will you earn?

3. Find the interest earned on an investment of $5,000 for 5 years compounded quarterly at 6%, 8%, 10%, 12%, and 15%.

4. If you wanted to retire in 30 years and have $100,000 to spend in a foolish manner, how much should you invest today at 12% compounded semiannually to earn your crazy money? What if you could invest at 12% compounded quarterly, how much would you need? How much would you need if it were monthly? Daily?

5. If you needed $15,000 in 20 years to send your firstborn on a trip to Tiro, Ohio, how much should you invest today at 11% compounded quarterly to reach your goal?

6. Which investment would be best—$10,000 at 12% compounded quarterly for 5 years, $10,000 at 11% quarterly for 6 years, $10,000 at 12% semimonthly for 5 years, or $9,000 at 13% compounded annually for 8 years?

7. Find the interest earned on $10,000 at 12% compounded monthly for 5 years, 10 years, 25 years, and 40 years. Put all of this information on one screen and print out the spreadsheet.

8. If you need $20,000 in 8 years, what would be the principal needed if you could invest at 6% annually, 8% annually, 10% annually, 18% annually, and finally 30% annually?

9. How much would you have in your savings account today if you had invested $5,000 at 18% compounded quarterly 15 years ago? How much interest would you have earned?

10. *Approximately* how many years will it take for an investment of $1,000 to double if it is invested at 8% compounded quarterly?

11. *Approximately* how many years will it take for an investment of $5,000 to double if it is invested at 8% compounded quarterly?

12. Compare your answers to Questions 10 and 11 above. What can you say about the time it takes for an investment to double?

13. Can the simple interest formula be used to calculate compound interest? Explain in a brief sentence.

14. Explain why compounding interest monthly yields more interest in one year than does compounding annually, assuming the interest rates are equal.

15. Put your cursor in cell F9 and record the contents of the cell. Write this "Excel" formula as a typical "math" formula and record it on the answer sheet.

PROJECT 6 ANSWERS

NAME_____   CLASS_____   HOUR_____

1. Annually_____   Semiannually_____

    Quarterly_____   Monthly_____   Daily_____

2._____

3. 6%_____   8%_____   10%_____

    12%_____   15%_____

4. Semiannually_____   Quarterly_____

    Monthly_____   Daily_____

5. _____

6. _____

7. Attach the printout. Circle the answer and label it as #7.

8. 6%_____   8%_____   10%_____

    18%_____   30%_____

9. Balance_____   Interest_____

10. _____

11._____

12. _____

13. _____

_____

14. _____

_____

15. _____   _____

MATHEMATICS USED IN PROJECT 6

The formula used for compound interest is a little more complicated than that for simple interest. However, it is based in the formula $P = BR$. There is not enough room on this page to show the relationship between $P = BR$ and the compound interest formula. In addition to knowing the principal P, interest rate R, and the time t in years, you also must know the number of times per year n that interest is added to the account, (compounded), as well as the interest rate per period r (called the periodic rate). If interest is compounded quarterly (4 times per year), then the periodic rate r is equal to the annual rate R divided by the number of compounding periods per year, 4. If interest is compounded monthly, then $r = \dfrac{R}{12}$, etc. Finally, you need to know the total number of compounding periods N for the duration of the investment. To find N, multiply the number of periods in one year by the number of years in the investment, $N = nt$.

The formula for the amount of interest plus principal, or the total value of the investment is

$$A = P(1+r)^N$$

where A is the dollar amount after t years.

Example 1: For an investment $P = \$10,000$ at an annual rate of $R = 12\%$ compounded quarterly for $t = 20$ years, the total amount of the investment is $A = 10000(1+.03)^{80}$,

where $r = \dfrac{12\%}{4} = 3\% = .03$, and $N = 20(4) = 80$.

Then $A = 10000(1+.03)^{80} = 10000(10.64089) = \$106,408.90$

Example 2: For an investment $P = \$6,500$ at an annual rate of $R = 9\%$ compounded monthly for $t = 10$ years,

$r = \dfrac{9\%}{12} = .75\% = .0075$, and $N = 10(12) = 120$.

The total value of the investment is:

$A = 6500(1+.0075)^{120} = 6500(2.4513572) = \$15,933.82$.

WHAT IF THE PROBLEM IS TURNED AROUND?

If you know the final amount of an investment and you would like to know what initial principal would generate this amount, you can use the same formula. Except the formula needs to be changed a little. Divide both sides of the equation $A = P(1+r)^N$ by the quantity $(1+r)^N$ to arrive at a formula for principal $P = \dfrac{A}{(1+r)^N}$.

> **Example 3:** If you need $100,000 in 20 years, how much should you invest today at 14% compounded semiannually to end up with $100,000 in 20 years?
>
> $$r = \frac{14\%}{2} = 7\% = .07 \qquad N = 20(2) = 40 \qquad A = \$100,000$$
>
> $$\text{Then} \quad P = \frac{A}{(1+r)^N}: \quad P = \frac{100000}{(1+.07)^{40}} = \frac{100000}{14.974458} = \$6,678.04$$

Thus, if you invested $6,678.04 today at 14% interest compounded semiannually you would have $100,000 in 20 years.

> **Example 4:** If the investment giant, Grab-It Inc. needed $20,000,000 in 5 years to grab up the Mighty Small Company, how much should the Grab-It Inc. Chief Financial Officer invest today at 38% interest compounded annually to be able to grab up the Mighty Small Company?
>
> $$r = \frac{38\%}{1} = 38\% = 0.38 \qquad N = 5(1) = 5 \qquad A = \$20,000,000$$
>
> $$\text{Then} \quad P = \frac{A}{(1+r)^N}: \quad P = \frac{20000000}{(1+.38)^5} = \frac{20000000}{5.0049003} = \$3,996,083.60$$

PROJECT 7
ANNUITIES

Sample Computer Screens

Project 7: Annuities Template ⟨Future Value Annuities⟩

Enter your name in the box to the right   Name: [   ]

Future Value Annuities

Deposit Amount	Annual Interest Rate	Number of Deposits per Year	Years	Future Value, Annuity Due	Future Value, Ordinary Annuity	Total Amount Deposited
$500.00	10.0%	12	15	$208,962.13	$207,235.17	$90,000.00
$400.00	11.0%	12	15	$183,543.03	$181,875.83	$72,000.00
$300.00	16.0%	12	25	$1,189,565.34	$1,173,913.17	$90,000.00
$200.00	15.0%	12	25	$656,814.75	$648,705.92	$60,000.00
$25.00	10.0%	12	40	$159,419.51	$158,101.99	$12,000.00
$1,425.00		TOTALS		$2,398,304.76	$2,369,832.08	$324,000.00

Sinking Fund Payments

Deposit Amount	Annual Interest Rate	Number of Payments per Year	Years	Desired Future Value of an Ordinary Annuity	Total of all Payments	Interest Earned
$244.09	10.0%	12	10	$50,000.00	$29,290.44	$20,709.56
$109.97	11.0%	12	15	$50,000.00	$19,793.72	$30,206.28
$28.96	16.0%	12	20	$50,000.00	$6,950.71	$43,049.29
$15.42	15.0%	12	25	$50,000.00	$4,624.59	$45,375.41
$14.31	12.0%	12	30	$50,000.00	$5,150.27	$44,849.73
$412.74		Totals		$250,000.00	$65,809.74	$184,190.26

Project 7: Annuities Template ⟨Present Value Annuities⟩

Enter your name in the box to the right   Name: [   ]

Present Value Annuities: Finding a payment amount

Payment Amount	Annual Interest Rate	Number of Payments per Year	Years	Present Value, Ordinary Annuity	Total of all Payments	Interest Earned
$500.00	10.0%	12	10	$37,835.58	$60,000.00	$22,164.42
$400.00	11.0%	12	15	$35,192.77	$72,000.00	$36,807.23
$300.00	16.0%	12	20	$21,563.25	$72,000.00	$50,436.75
$200.00	15.0%	12	25	$15,614.87	$60,000.00	$44,385.13
$25.00	10.0%	12	30	$2,848.77	$9,000.00	$6,151.23
$1,425.00		TOTALS		$113,055.24	$273,000.00	$159,944.76

Present Value Annuities: Finding the present value

Payment Amount	Annual Interest Rate	Number of Payments per Year	Years	Present Value, Ordinary Annuity	Total of all Payments	Interest Earned
$660.75	10.0%	12	10	$50,000.00	$79,290.44	$29,290.44
$568.30	11.0%	12	15	$50,000.00	$102,293.72	$52,293.72
$695.63	16.0%	12	20	$50,000.00	$166,950.71	$116,950.71
$640.42	15.0%	12	25	$50,000.00	$192,124.59	$142,124.59
$514.31	12.0%	12	30	$50,000.00	$185,150.27	$135,150.27
$3,079.40		Totals		$250,000.00	$725,809.74	$475,809.74

DIRECTIONS:

1. Please read all directions. Study and analyze the computer screens before you start answering the questions. Most questions will require information from the computer screens.

2. Open Project 7 by selecting Project_07 on your hard drive or floppy disk (In Excel use File, Open). Set the *zoom* percentage for your screen resolution. For 640 by 480 pixels use a *zoom* setting of 55%, for a screen resolution of 800 by 600 pixels use a *zoom* setting of 75%, and for a screen resolution of 1024 by 768 pixels or higher use a *zoom* setting of 100%.

3. Project 7 contains two spreadsheets, Future Value Annuities and Present Value Annuities. Use the tabs in the lower left corner of the worksheet to move between spreadsheets.

4. When you enter numeric data, do not include the $ or the , in the number. For example, to enter $1,765.56 you should enter 1765.56. To enter a percentage you must enter the value in decimal form. To enter an interest rate of 5% you must type .05. Only values in blue can be changed.

5. If you need to reset the data to the original values for Project 7—as in the sample screens above—simply **reopen the project** by clicking on the Excel commands File, Open and then select Project_07 followed by clicking on yes.

6. To print a copy of the spreadsheet, select the print icon from the top toolbar.

PROJECT 7 QUESTIONS

If you have not already done so, reset the information using the sample screens at the beginning of this project.

1. Suppose that when you were 18 years old you started depositing $20 at the end of each month in a mutual fund that paid 17% compounded monthly. If you continue to do this until you are 65 years old, how much money will you have in your mutual fund at ages 40, 50, 60, and 65? Is this an ordinary annuity or an annuity due?

2. If you could either deposit $400 per month in one ordinary annuity at 11% compounded monthly, or deposit the $400 in four separate $100 per month ordinary annuities at 11% compounded monthly, which would generate more money after 30 years?

3. Find the value of an ordinary annuity and an annuity due of $2,000 per year at 18% compounded annually for 30 years. Why is the annuity due larger?

4. Find the future value and the total amount deposited for the following ordinary annuities:
    a. $100 per month at 14% compounded monthly for 30 years.
    b. $300 per quarter at 14% compounded quarterly for 30 years.
    c. $600 every 6 months at 14% compounded semiannually for 30 years.
    d. $1,200 per year at 14% compounded annually for 30 years.

5. How much must be deposited each month at 8% compounded monthly in order to have $100,000 in 10 years and in 20 years? When the time period doubles, are the sinking fund payments cut in half? Why?

6. You want to save money to buy a new car in 4 years. How much should you deposit at the end of each month in an account that pays 9% interest compounded monthly in order to have $40,000 in 4 years?

7. Sam deposits $250 at the end of each month in an annuity that pays 16% compounded monthly. Jackie deposits $750 at the end of each quarter in an annuity that pays 16% compounded quarterly. How much money will each of them invest over a 10-year period? Who will have more money in their account after 10 years? Explain.

8. Use the Present Value Annuity spreadsheet to determine the present value of an annuity that pays $1,000 a month for 10 years, 15 years, and 20 years, at an annual rate of 8%.

9. Suppose that when you retire you are able to deposit $1,000,000 in an annuity with an annual interest rate of 18% compounded monthly. This annuity will then pay you a fixed amount each month. What will the monthly payment be if the term of the annuity is 10 years, 15 years, and 25 years?

10. Fixed rate loans are a form of present value annuity in which the lending institution has paid you the present value of the annuity and your monthly loan payments are the annuity payment. If you borrow $40,000 at 9% compounded monthly for 4 years, what will your monthly payment be? How much will you pay over the life of this loan? How does this present value annuity compare with the future value annuity from Question 6 above?

11. Which of the following annuities pays the greatest amount of interest? An ordinary future value annuity with a future value of $75,000 and an interest rate of 20% compounded monthly over 10 years; or a present value annuity with an interest rate of 20% compounded monthly and a 10 year payment schedule, if the present value of the annuity is $75,000? Explain.

12. Put your cursor in cell G17 and record the contents of the cell. Write this "Excel" formula as a typical "math" formula and record it on the answer sheet.

PROJECT 7 ANSWERS

NAME_____   CLASS_____   HOUR_____

1.   Age 40_____   Age 50_____

      Age 60_____   Age 65_____

2.   _____

3.   Ordinary_____   Annuity due_____

      _____

4.   a._____   b._____

      c._____   d._____

5.   _____

6.   _____

7.   Sam_____   Jackie_____

      Explain _____

8.   10 Year_____   15 Year_____   20 Year_____

9.   10 Year_____   15 Year_____   25 Year_____

10.   Payment_____   Total paid_____

      _____

11.   _____

      _____

12.   _____   _____

MATHEMATICS USED IN PROJECT 7

Suppose that when you retire, you would like to have saved several hundred thousand dollars. One way of getting this money is to make small monthly payments over a long period of time. Another method is to already have a large sum of money. Most of us do not have a great amount of money to invest, but we can usually manage to invest a small amount. If you can do this on a regular basis and for a long period of time, you will end up with a large sum of money. When you invest money on a regular schedule, it is called an annuity.

To calculate the future value of your annuity will require several keystrokes on your calculator. To make the keystrokes simpler, there are two intermediate steps. Calculate the periodic interest rate i, and the total number of deposits N (also called payments). The periodic rate is the annual rate divided by the number (n) of deposits or payments per year.

$$i = \frac{annual\ rate}{n}$$

The total number of deposits (payments) in the annuity is the number n per year times the number of years t in the life of the annuity.

$$N = n \times t$$

The deposits (payments) must be made at the same time intervals as the compounding periods. The value of the annuity is

$$A = R * \frac{(1+i)^N - 1}{i} = \frac{R}{i} * \left((1+i)^N - 1\right)$$

where i = the periodic interest rate

       R = the amount of the regular deposit

       N = total number of deposits

For example, if you deposit \$100 each month at 12% annual interest compounded monthly for 30 years, you will have \$349,496.39 in 30 years. This is called the future value of the annuity.

$$i = \frac{.12}{12} = 0.01 \quad N = 12*30 = 360$$

$$A = \frac{100}{0.01} \left((1+0.01)^{360} - 1\right)$$

The keystrokes are 100   ÷   .01   *   ((1   +   .01   )   ^   360   –   1   )   =

Note that the ^ symbol is the same as y^x. They both mean exponentiation.

PROJECT 8
INSTALLMENT LOANS

Sample Computer Screens

Project 8: Installment Loans and APR Template

Enter your name in the box to the right   Name: [   ]

Installment Price and APR

Cash Price	Finance Charge	Down Payment	Total Number of Payments	Installment Price	Monthly Payment Amount	APR
$500.00	$25.00	$20.00	12	$525.00	$42.08	9.48%
$1,000.00	$125.00	$50.00	18	$1,125.00	$59.72	16.02%
$1,800.00	$150.00	$0.00	18	$1,950.00	$108.33	10.28%
$2,735.00	$200.00	$750.00	24	$2,935.00	$91.04	9.39%

Refund of Finance Charges, Rule of 78

Finance Charge	Original Number of Payments	Number of Payments Remaining	Refund Fraction	Refund of Finance Charges
$125.00	6	3	2/7	$35.71
$200.00	12	6	7/26	$53.85
$300.00	12	3	1/13	$23.08
$50.00	18	8	4/19	$10.53

DIRECTIONS:

1. Please read all directions. Study and analyze the computer screen before you start answering the questions. Most questions will require information from the computer screens.

2. Open Project 8 by selecting Project_08 on your hard drive or floppy disk (In Excel use File, Open). Set the *zoom* percentage for your screen resolution. For 640 by 480 pixels use a *zoom* setting of 55%, for a screen resolution of 800 by 600 pixels use a *zoom* setting of 75%, and for a screen resolution of 1024 by 768 pixels or higher use a *zoom* setting of 100%.

3. Project 8 contains one spreadsheet.

4. When you enter numeric data, do not include the $ or the , in the number. For example, to enter $1,765.56 you should enter 1765.56. To enter a percentage you must enter the value in decimal form. To enter an interest rate of 5% you must type .05. Only cell values in blue can be changed.

5. If you need to reset the data to the original values for Project 8—as in the sample screens above—simply **reopen the project** by clicking on the Excel commands File, Open and then select Project_08 followed by clicking on yes.

6. To print a copy of the spreadsheet, select the print icon from the top toolbar.

PROJECT 8 QUESTIONS

If you have not already done so, reset the information using the sample screens at the beginning of this project.

1. What is the installment price and monthly payment required to purchase a plasma screen television with a cash price of $6,340, if the installment plan calls for a down payment of $200, finance charges of $850, and 18 equal monthly payments?

2. What is the annual percentage rate for the installment loan in Question 1 above?

3. The consumer in Question 1 above decided to pay off the installment loan in the 12th month. Use the Rule of 78 to determine how much of the $850 finance charge would be refunded to him.

4. Smart-Shop offers two installment plans for their customers. Under Plan A an item with a cash price of $2,000 can be purchased with a down payment of $500, $250 in finance charges, and 12 equal monthly payments. Under Plan B the same item can be purchased with a down payment of $100, finance charges of $400 and 24 equal monthly payments. What is the installment price, monthly payment, and APR for each plan? Which is the better plan in your opinion? Why?

5. You need to buy a new refrigerator. The model you have selected has a cash price of $1,340 and is offered on an installment plan that requires a minimum down payment of $50, finance charges of 12% of the cash price minus the down payment, and 12 equal monthly payments. What is the installment price, the monthly payment, and the APR for this installment plan?

6. For the purchase in Question 5 above, what are the new installment price, monthly payment, and APR if you decide to make a down payment of $300 rather than the $50 minimum? Note, you must recalculate the finance charge. (Do not replace the information you entered into the spreadsheet for Question 5)

7. What is the refund fraction and refund of finance charges for the installment loan in Question 5 above if you decide to pay off the installment loan after 6 months? After 8 months? After 10 months?

8. You want to redecorate your home and plan to purchase the following items on installment plans.

Item	Cash Price	Down Payment	Finance Charge	Number of Payments
Leather Sofa	$3,200	$50	$800	24
End Tables	$800	$0	$40	12
Entertainment System	$5,680	$250	$1,020	18
Recliner	$1,100	$100	$150	12

Enter the information for each of these installment loans in a different row on the spreadsheet. What are the monthly payments and installment prices for each loan? What is the total of all four monthly payments?

9. For the items purchased in Question 8 above, what is the total refund of finance charges if you pay off all of these installment loans after 9 months?

10. Print a copy of the spreadsheet with the information from Questions 8 and 9 and attach it to your answer page.

PROJECT 8 ANSWERS

NAME_____   CLASS_____   HOUR_____

1.   Installment price_____   Monthly payment_____

2.   Annual percentage rate_____

3.   Refund of finance charges_____

4.   Plan A installment price_____   Plan B installment price_____

     Plan A monthly payment_____   Plan B monthly payment_____

     Plan A APR _____   Plan B APR _____

     Better plan? Why?_____

     _____

5.   Installment price_____   Monthly payment_____

     Annual percentage rate_____

6.   Installment price_____   Monthly payment_____

     Annual percentage rate_____

7.   6 month refund fraction_____   Refund of finance charges_____

     8 month refund fraction_____   Refund of finance charges_____

     10 month refund fraction_____   Refund of finance charges_____

8.   Sofa installment price_____   Payment_____

     Tables installment price_____   Payment_____

     System installment price_____   Payment_____

     Recliner installment price_____   Payment_____

     Total installment price_____   Payment_____

9.   Total refund of finance charges_____

10. Attach your printout of the spreadsheet.

MATHEMATICS USED IN PROJECT 8

In Project 8 we look at the mathematics of consumer credit. For an installment loan the governing equation is the relationship between the cash price, the finance charge (or interest), and the installment price of the item being purchased.

$$\text{Installment Price} = \text{Cash Price} + \text{Finance Charges}$$

The regular monthly installment payment amount can be calculated by subtracting the down payment from the installment price and then dividing the result by the number of payments to be made.

$$\text{Monthly Payment} = \frac{\text{Installment Price} - \text{Down Payment}}{\text{Number of scheduled payments}}$$

The annual percentage rate (APR) provides a means for consumers to compare different loan options. The lower the APR is the less the consumer is paying for the loan. APR is particularly valuable in comparing installment loans since often the finance charges are stated as a flat dollar amount rather than a percentage of the credit extended. The calculation of the APR is very complicated. It is essentially the effective annual percentage rate discussed in the study of compound interest, but because the loan balance changes monthly, the effective rate must be considered as being applied to an annuity. Fortunately Excel has an effective rate formula built into the software design which calculates the APR for us. Without this formula we could approximate the APR using what is known as the constant ratio formula.

Constant Ratio Formula for APR:

$$\text{APR} \approx \frac{2 \times \text{the number of payments in 1 year} \times \text{finance charge}}{\text{amount financed} \times (\text{total number of payments} + 1)}$$

Another aspect of installment loans is the refund of finance charges when the consumer decides to pay off their installment loan early. Because the loan balance is higher when the loan is first issued than it is when the loan is closer to being paid off, the finance charges are higher at the beginning of the loan's term than they are at the end. The generally accepted formula for determining the refund of finance charges for an early payoff is known as the Rule of 78.

Rule of 78:

$$\text{Refund of finance charges} = \text{Total finance charges} \times \text{refund fraction}$$

Where the refund fraction is:

$$\text{Refund Fraction} = \frac{1 + 2 + 3 + \cdots + \text{number of payments remaining}}{1 + 2 + 3 + \cdots + \text{total number of payments}}$$

Since $1 + 2 + 3 + 4 + 5 + 6 + 7 + 8 + 9 + 10 + 11 + 12 = 78$ and most installment loans have a 12-month term, the denominator of the refund fraction is very often 78. Hence the name, "Rule of 78."

Sample Computer Screens

Project 9: Mortgages, Loans, and Amortization Templates

Enter your name in the box to the right   Name: [   ]

Finding Monthly Payments and Interest Totals

Mortgage or Loan Amount	Annual Interest Rate	Mortgage or Loan Term (in years)	Monthly Payment	Total of all Payments	Total Interest Paid
$108,000.00	3.25%	30	$470.02	$169,208.22	$61,208.22
$15,265.00	7.50%	5	$305.88	$18,352.76	$3,087.76
$25,500.00	5.00%	10	$270.47	$32,456.05	$6,956.05
$30,000.00	4.00%	10	$303.74	$36,448.25	$6,448.25

$178,765.00	Totals		$1,350.10	$256,465.27	$77,700.27

Finding Loan Amounts for a Fixed Payment

Mortgage or Loan Amount	Annual Interest Rate	Mortgage or Loan Term (in years)	Monthly Payment	Total of all Payments	Total Interest Paid
$17,995.54	6.25%	5	$350.00	$21,000.00	$3,004.46

Project 9: Mortgages, Loans, and Amortization Templates

Enter your name in the box to the right   Name: [   ]

Mortgage or Loan Amount	Annual Interest Rate	Mortgage or Loan Term (in years)	Monthly Payment	Total of all Payments	Total Interest Paid
$120,000.00	4.00%	30	$572.90	$206,243.41	$86,243.41

Amortization Schedule

Scroll Down to see the Complete Amortization Schedule	Month	Payment Amount	Portion of Payment applied to Interest	Portion of Payment applied to Principal	Outstanding Balance
	0				$120,000.00
	1	$572.90	$400.00	$172.90	$119,827.10
	2	$572.90	$399.42	$173.47	$119,653.63
	3	$572.90	$398.85	$174.05	$119,479.57
	4	$572.90	$398.27	$174.63	$119,304.94

49

DIRECTIONS:

1. Please read all directions. Study and analyze the computer screens before you start answering the questions. Most questions will require information from the computer screens.

2. Open Project 9 by selecting Project_09 on your hard drive or floppy disk (In Excel use File, Open). Set the *zoom* percentage for your screen resolution. For 640 by 480 pixels use a *zoom* setting of 55%, for a screen resolution of 800 by 600 pixels use a *zoom* setting of 75%, and for a screen resolution of 1024 by 768 pixels or higher use a *zoom* setting of 100%.

3. Project 9 contains two spreadsheets: the first spreadsheet is titled Payments and Interest, and the second is titled Amortization Schedule. Use the tabs in the lower left corner of the spreadsheet to move between spreadsheets.

4. When you enter numeric data, do not include the $ or the , in the number. For example, to enter $1,765.56 you should enter 1765.56. To enter a percentage you must enter the value in decimal form. To enter an interest rate of 5% you must type .05. Only cell values in blue can be changed.

5. If you need to reset the data to the original values for Project 9—as in the sample screens above—simply **reopen the project** by clicking on the Excel commands File, Open and then select Project_09 followed by clicking on yes.

6. To print a copy of the spreadsheet, select the print icon from the top toolbar. The Amortization spreadsheet will not fit on one page, because this spreadsheet is eight pages long.

PROJECT 9 QUESTIONS

If you have not already done so, reset the information using the sample screens at the beginning of this project.

1. If you borrow $10,000 at 10.5% for 4 years, what will be the monthly payment, the total interest paid by you, and the total paid back by you?

2. Which loan will cost more, a $5,000 loan at 12% for 3 years or a $4,700 loan at 12% for 4 years? The cost of a loan is the total interest paid.

3. If you buy a house with a mortgage of $100,000 at 8.9% for 30 years, how much will your total payments be over the 30 year period? How much of the total payments will be interest?

4. For a loan of $25,000 at 11% for 10 years, use the amortization spreadsheet to determine in which month of the loan the portion of the monthly payment that goes toward principal will be greater than the portion that pays interest.

5. If you need to buy a car and you can only afford a payment of $175.00 per month, approximately how much could you borrow if the time on the loan is 4 years and the rate is 9%?

6. Find the monthly payment and the total interest paid on the following loans:

	Principal	Rate	Time (in years)
a.	$25,000	10.5%	7
b.	$31,000	10%	10
c.	$12,000	9.8%	4
d.	$5,000	11%	2

7. For a $20,000 loan at 12%, find a time (in months) that will yield a monthly payment of approximately $300.

8. What is the difference in total interest paid on loans of $15,000 at 11% for 4 years and $15,000 at 11% for 5 years? What is the difference in the monthly payment for these loans?

9. What is the difference in total interest paid on loans of $70,000 at 12% for 30 years and $70,000 at 12% for 25 years? What is the difference in the monthly payment for these loans?

10. Using the Amortization Schedule spreadsheet on a loan of $75,000 at 10% for 30 years and your calculator, find the total interest paid in the first 5 years, then in the second 5 years and in the third and finally in the fourth 5 years.

11. Using the results from Question 10, why is the interest paid in the first 5 years greater than any other group of 5 years?

12. If you want to buy a home with a price of $180,000 and the current interest rate is 5% for 30 years; how much money can be saved over the life of the loan by making a down payment of 20% of the price of the house over a 10% down payment? Note the down payment will reduce the amount of the mortgage.

13. You have just graduated from college and found a job in your field. You bought a house and have a 30 year mortgage of $103,500 at 6%, you have student loans totaling $26,000 at 4.5% for 10 years, a car loan of $18,350 at 7.5% for 5 years, and a personal credit loan of $5,000 at 9% for 2 years. What is your total indebtedness, what is the total of your monthly loan payments, and how much interest will you have paid when all of these loans have been paid off?

14. Put your cursor in cell E13 in the Amortization spreadsheet and record the contents of the cell. Write this "Excel" formula as a typical "math" formula and record it on the answer sheet.

PROJECT 9 ANSWERS

NAME_____   CLASS_____   HOUR_____

1. Monthly payment_____   Total interest_____   Total paid_____

2. Circle the correct answer: $5,000 $4,700

3. Total cost _____   Interest_____

4. Month_____

5. Amount borrowed_____

6. Payment   a)_____   b)_____   c)_____   d)_____

    Interest   a)_____   b)_____   c)_____   d)_____

7. Time_____

8. Interest difference_____   Payment difference _____

9. Interest difference_____   Payment difference _____

10. Total interest, first 5 years_____   Total interest, second 5 years_____

    Total interest, third 5 years_____   Total interest, fourth 5 years_____

11. _____

12. Savings _____

13. Total indebtedness_____   Total payment_____

    Total interest_____

14. _____   _____

MATHEMATICS USED IN PROJECT 9

The mathematics of Project 9 is a combination of the present value annuity formulas from Project 7 and the simple interest mathematics found in Project 5. That is, to calculate the interest paid for any month, the simple interest formula $I = PRT$ is used. The principal is the outstanding balance, the rate is the stated annual rate, and the time is 1/12 of a year (1 month). The portion paid to reduce the principal balance each month is the amount of the monthly payment minus the amount of simple interest. The monthly payment is calculated from the same formula that was used in Project 7. However, this time the calculation $\dfrac{R}{12}$ will be called i because it is the periodic interest rate.

$$monthly\ payment = \frac{P \times i}{1 - (i+1)^{-12t}}$$

where R = annual Rate, P = Principal, $i = \dfrac{R}{12}$, and t = time in years.

For example, let P = \$9,000.00, R = 10% (thus $i = \dfrac{.1}{12} = .00833333$), t = 3 years (36 months). Thus, for a \$9,000 loan at 10% compounded monthly for 3 years, the monthly payment is \$290.40. We can calculate the total amount paid by multiplying the payment amount by the number of payments to be made. Total paid = $\$290.40 \times 12 \times 3 = \$10,454.40$. Then we can determine the total interest paid by subtracting the original loan amount from the total amount of all payments.

Total interest = \$10,454.40 – \$9,000.00 = \$1,454.40

The computer makes an amortization schedule using the argument that follows: For the first month the interest is $9000 \times .1 \times \dfrac{1}{12} = 75$ (from $I = PRT$). The amount of the payment that is applied to the principal then is found by subtracting the monthly interest from the payment, \$290.40 – \$75.00 = \$215.40. The outstanding principal balance after the payment is made is found by subtracting the payment's principal amount from the principal balance, \$9,000.00 – \$215.40 = \$8,784.60.

At this point the calculations for month 2 can be carried out:

interest = $\$8748.60 \times .1 \times \dfrac{1}{12} = \$73.21$; principal = \$290.40 – 73.21 = \$217.19;

and the outstanding principal balance = \$8,784.60 – \$217.19 = \$8,567.41.

And so the calculations go on month after month until the outstanding balance has been reduced to zero. It is interesting to note that each month the interest portion of the payment is lower because the outstanding principal balance has been reduced and so the principal portion of the payment is greater.

PROJECT 10
DEPRECIATION

Sample Computer Screens

Project 10: Depreciation Templates

Enter your name in the box to the right   Name: [   ]

Asset Information:

Total Cost	$50,000.00
Expected Life (in years)	6
Salvage Value	$3,000.00
Total Depreciation	$47,000.00

Depreciation Schedule: Straight-Line Method

Year	Rate	Depreciation	Accumulated Depreciation	Book Value
0		$0.00	$0.00	$50,000.00
1	1/6	$7,833	$7,833	$42,167
2	1/6	$7,833	$15,667	$34,333
3	1/6	$7,833	$23,500	$26,500
4	1/6	$7,833	$31,333	$18,667
5	1/6	$7,833	$39,167	$10,833
6	1/6	$7,833	$47,000	$3,000
7				
8				
9				
10				
11				
12				

DIRECTIONS:

1. Please read all directions. Study and analyze the computer screens before you start answering the questions. Most questions will require information from the computer screens.

2. Open Project 10 by selecting Project_10 on your hard drive or floppy disk (In Excel use File, Open). Set the *zoom* percentage for your screen resolution. For 640 by 480 pixels use a *zoom* setting of 55%, for a screen resolution of 800 by 600 pixels use a *zoom* setting of 75%, and for a screen resolution of 1024 by 768 pixels or higher use a *zoom* setting of 100%.

3. Project 10 contains 6 spreadsheets: Straight-Line Method, Sum-of-the-Years-Digits Method, Double-Declining-Balance Method, MACRS Method, MACRS rate tables, and a Graphic. Select the appropriate spreadsheet by using the tabs in the lower part of the screen.

4. When you enter numeric data, do not include the $ or the , in the number. For example, to enter $1,765.56 you should enter 1765.56. Only cell values in blue can be changed.

5. If you need to reset the data to the original values for Project 10—as in the sample screens above—simply **reopen the project** by clicking on the Excel commands File, Open and then select Project_10 followed by clicking on yes.

6. To print a copy of the spreadsheet, select the print icon from the top toolbar.

7. To close this project and continue working in Excel, select the *close* option under the File menu. To exit Excel completely click on the X in the upper right corner of the screen. Do not save your work.

PROJECT 10 QUESTIONS

If you have not already done so, reset the information using the sample screens at the beginning of this project.

1. For each of the four methods of depreciation, find the depreciation, accumulated depreciation, and book value in year 4 for equipment costing $20,000, with an estimated life of 7 years and a salvage value of $2,000.

2. Rework Question 1 for year 5, when cost = $10,000, life = 6 years, and salvage value = $1,000.

3. Print out a depreciation schedule for the following assets:

   a. Cost = $6,000, life = 8 years, salvage value = $500, sum-of-the-years-digits method.

   b. Cost = $18,000, life = 5 years, salvage value = $2,000, double declining-balance method.

   c. Cost = $25,000, life = 3 years, salvage value = $4,000, straight-line method.

   d. Cost = $20,000, life = 5 years, MACRS method.

4. For an asset with a cost of $28,000, an estimated life of 10 years, and salvage value of $4,000, find the first year in which the accumulated depreciation exceeds the book value when using the double declining balance method.

5. For each of the depreciation methods, enter $25,000 for the cost, 10 years for the life, and $6,000 for the salvage value. Then go to the Graphics spreadsheet and study the graph of book value versus year. Which method's graph drops off the fastest? Which method's graph seems the most different? How is it different?

6. For each of the depreciation methods, enter $75,000 for the cost, 7 years for the life, and $16,000 for the salvage value. If you have to pay tax based on the current value of your assets, which method of depreciation would result in the lowest tax cost for the third year of the asset's life? Which would cost the most?

7. For each of the depreciation methods, enter $50,000 for the cost, 10 years for the life, and $4,000 for the salvage value. If your business was destroyed in a fire and the insurance company will only pay you the book value of your assets at the time of the fire, which method would result in the largest insurance settlement? Which would result in the lowest? How do your answers to this question compare to your answers to Question 6?

8. If the cost of an asset is the same as the salvage value, can depreciation be claimed?

9. If the estimated life of an asset is 0 years, how much depreciation can be claimed?

10. If your business is "given" some equipment with a value of $10,000, do you think you can claim any depreciation?

11. After observing the graph of straight-line depreciation in Question 5, propose a reason as to how it got the name straight-line depreciation.

12. Using the Straight-Line Depreciation spreadsheet, put your cursor in cell E9 and record the contents of the cell. Write this "Excel" formula as a typical "math" formula and record it on the answer sheet.

PROJECT 10 ANSWERS

NAME_____   CLASS_____   HOUR_____

1.
                      Depreciation   Total depreciation   Book value
    Straight line: _____   _____   _____

    Declining balance:_____   _____   _____

    Sum-of-years: _____   _____   _____

    MACRS: _____   _____   _____

2.
                      Depreciation   Total depreciation   Book value
    Straight line: _____   _____   _____

    Declining balance:_____   _____   _____

    Sum-of-years: _____   _____   _____

    MACRS: _____   _____   _____

3. Label the answers and attach the printouts to this sheet.

4. Year_____

5. _____

    _____

6. _____

    _____

7. _____

    _____

8. _____

9. _____

10._____

11. _____

12. _____   _____

MATHEMATICS USED IN PROJECT 10

Depreciation is the loss of value of an asset due to use or age. In business, an asset's depreciation can be claimed on the company's year-end tax statements as a tax credit. Because of this, it is important to standardize the ways in which a business may calculate an asset's depreciation. This project illustrates four of the most commonly accepted methods for calculating depreciation.

Regardless of the depreciation method used, the total depreciation is the difference between the cost of the asset and the asset's expected salvage value. Salvage value is the anticipated value of the asset at the end of its depreciation life.

Total Depreciation = Cost − Salvage Value

The accumulated depreciation of an asset is the total of all annual depreciation amounts claimed thus far.

Accumulated Depreciation = Previous accumulated depreciation + current annual depreciation

The *Book Value* of an asset is the value assigned to that asset for that year.

Book value = Cost − Accumulated Depreciation

These aspects of depreciation are then organized in a table called a depreciation schedule.

STRAIGHT-LINE DEPRECIATION:

Using the straight-line depreciation method, the depreciation for each year is found by dividing the asset's *total depreciation* by the asset's e*stimated life*.

> **Example**: For an asset with a *Cost* = $2,000, and an estimated *Life* = 5 years, and a *Salvage Value* = $200.
>
> *Total Depreciation* = $2,000 − $200 = $1,800 .
>
> And so *Annual Depreciation* = $1,800 ÷ 5 = $360
>
> Thus the depreciation for each year of the estimated life of the equipment is $360.

DOUBLE-DECLINING-BALANCE DEPRECIATION

Under this depreciation the amount of depreciation that can be claimed early in the assets life is greater than the straight-line method amounts. Annual depreciation is found by multiplying the depreciation rate by the previous year's book value. The depreciation rate is

$$Rate = \frac{2}{estimated\ life}$$

However, the accumulated depreciation may never be larger than *total depreciation* and so the accountant must be careful not to claim more depreciation than the asset is entitled to.

Example: Using the data in the previous example:

$$First\ Year's\ Depreciation = \left(\frac{2}{5}\right) \times \$2000 = .4 \times \$2000 = \$800,$$

The book value at the end of the first year is

$$Book\ Value = \$2000 - \$800 = \$1,200.$$

$$Second\ Year's\ Depreciation = \left(\frac{2}{5}\right) \times \$1200 = .4 \times \$1200 = \$480$$

The book value at the end of the second year is

$$Book\ Value = \$1200 - \$480 = \$720.$$

$$Third\ Year's\ Depreciation = \left(\frac{2}{5}\right) \times \$720 = .4 \times \$720 = \$288$$

The book value at the end of the third year is

$$Book\ Value = \$720 - \$288 = \$432.$$

$$Fourth\ Year's\ Depreciation = \left(\frac{2}{5}\right) \times \$432 = .4 \times \$432 = \$173$$

Notice depreciation is always rounded to the nearest whole dollar.

The book value at the end of the fourth year is

$$Book\ Value = \$432 - \$173 = \$259.$$

Following the fourth year of depreciation the accumulated depreciation is $800 + $480 + $288 + $173 = 1741. The most depreciation that may be claimed in this final year then is $1800 - $1741 = 59 in order to keep the accumulated depreciation from exceeding the total depreciation of $1,800.

SUM-OF-THE-YEARS-DIGITS DEPRECIATION

Like the Double-Declining-Balance Method, the depreciation for any given year is calculated using a depreciation rate. Unlike the previous method, however, the rate changes each year and the new rate is multiplied by the total depreciation rather than the previous book value. The depreciation rate is a fraction whose denominator is the sum of the digits from 1 through the estimated life of the asset and whose numerator is one more than the asset's estimated life minus the depreciation year.

Example: Using the same data:

The asset has an estimated useful life of 5 years so the depreciation rate fraction will have a denominator of $1 + 2 + 3 + 4 + 5 = 15$.

A table of depreciation rates for this asset would be:

Depreciation Year	1	2	3	4	5
Depreciation Rate	$\dfrac{5}{15}$	$\dfrac{4}{15}$	$\dfrac{3}{15}$	$\dfrac{2}{15}$	$\dfrac{1}{15}$

And so

$$First\ Year's\ Depreciation = \left(\frac{5}{15}\right) \times \$1800 = \$600\ ,$$

The book value at the end of the first year is

$$Book\ Value = \$2000 - \$600 = \$1,400\ .$$

$$Second\ Year's\ Depreciation = \left(\frac{4}{15}\right) \times \$1800 = \$480$$

The book value at the end of the second year is

$$Book\ Value = \$1400 - \$480 = \$920\ .$$

And so forth until the end of the asset's depreciation life.

MODIFIED ACCELERATED COST RECOVERY SYSTEM (MACRS) DEPRECIATION

The MACRS method is a method of determining an asset's depreciation based on a table of depreciation rates provided by the government. Under this method, the annual depreciation is found by looking up the depreciation rate for the year and multiplying that rate by the original cost of the asset. This method is unique in that it allows the business to depreciate an asset's value to $0.

Example: Using the same data:

The asset has an estimated useful life of 5 years so the depreciation rates

can be found from the MACRS table.

A table of depreciation rates for this asset would be:

Depreciation Year	1	2	3	4	5	6
Depreciation Rate	0.2000	0.3200	0.1920	0.1152	0.1152	0.0576

Notice that an asset with a 5 year life is actually depreciated over 6 years.

$First\ Year's\ Depreciation = .2000 \times \$2000 = \$400$,

The book value at the end of the first year is

$Book\ Value = \$2000 - \$400 = \$1,600$.

$Second\ Year's\ Depreciation = .3200 \times \$2000 = \$640$

The book value at the end of the second year is

$Book\ Value = \$1600 - \$640 = \$960$.

And so forth until the end of the asset's depreciation life. At the end of the sixth year the book value of the asset is $0.

Sample Computer Screens

Project 11: Inventory Methods Templates

Enter your name in the box to the right   Name: [   ]

Specific Identification Method

Purchase Record

Date of Purchase	Number of Units Purchased	Cost per Unit	Total Cost	Number of Units in Ending Inventory	Cost of Units in Ending Inventory
Beginning Inventory	42	$2.42	$101.64	5	$12.10
July 7, 2003	16	$2.65	$42.40	3	$7.95
July 21, 2003	10	$2.75	$27.50	4	$11.00
August 4, 2003	18	$2.50	$45.00	8	$20.00
August 18, 2003	12	$2.45	$29.40	6	$14.70
August 30, 2003	6	$2.80	$16.80	5	$14.00

Total Number of Units Purchased	104	Total Cost of Units Purchased	$262.74	Total Cost of Ending Inventory	$79.75

Cost of Goods Sold	$182.99

Project 11: Inventory Methods Templates

Enter your name in the box to the right   Name: [   ]

Average Cost, FIFO, and LIFO Methods

Purchase Record

Date of Purchase	Number of Units Purchased	Cost per Unit	Total Cost
Beginning Inventory	42	$2.42	$101.64
July 7, 2003	16	$2.65	$42.40
July 21, 2003	10	$2.75	$27.50
August 4, 2003	18	$2.50	$45.00
August 18, 2003	12	$2.45	$29.40
August 30, 2003	6	$2.80	$16.80

Total Number of Units Purchased	104	Total Cost of Units	$262.74

Number of Units in Ending Inventory	31

Weighted Average Cost per Unit	$2.526

Method of Inventory Valuation	Cost of Ending Inventory	Cost of Goods Sold
Weighted Average Cost	$78.32	$184.42
First In First Out (FIFO)	$78.70	$184.04
Last In First Out (LIFO)	$75.02	$187.72

DIRECTIONS:

1. Please read all directions. Study and analyze the computer screen before you start answering the questions. Most questions will require information from the computer screens.

2. Open Project 11 by selecting Project_11 on your hard drive or floppy disk (In Excel use File, Open). Set the *zoom* percentage for your screen resolution. For 640 by 480 pixels use a *zoom* setting of 55%, for a screen resolution of 800 by 600 pixels use a *zoom* setting of 75%, and for a screen resolution of 1024 by 768 pixels or higher use a *zoom* setting of 100%.

3. Project 11 contains two spreadsheets. Each spreadsheet displays an item's purchase record and information necessary to determine the value of the ending inventory and the cost of goods sold. The first spreadsheet is titled Specific Identification and the second is titled Avg. Cost, FIFO, LIFO.

4. When you enter numeric data, do not include the $ or the , in the number. For example, to enter $1,765.56 you should enter 1765.56. Only cell values in blue can be changed.

5. If you need to reset the data to the original values for Project 11—as in the sample screens above—simply **reopen the project** by clicking on the Excel commands File, Open and then select Project_11 followed by clicking on yes.

6. To print a copy of the spreadsheet, select the print icon from the top toolbar.

7. To close this project and continue working in Excel, select the *close* option under the File menu. To exit Excel completely click on the X in the upper right corner of the screen. Do not save your work to disk.

PROJECT 11 QUESTIONS

If you have not already done so, reset the information using the sample screens at the beginning of this project.

1. If all of the units from the beginning, July 7, and July 21 purchases and 3 units from the August 4 purchase were sold but none of the units from the August 18 and August 30 purchases were sold, then what would be the value of the remaining inventory using the specific identification method?

2. Record the number of units remaining in inventory from Question 1 above. Enter this as the number of units in ending inventory on the Average Cost, FIFO, and LIFO spreadsheet. What is the value of the ending inventory and the cost of goods sold under each of these methods?

3. In Questions 1 and 2 above, why did the Specific Identification and FIFO methods result in the same inventory valuation?

4. On the Average Cost, FIFO, and LIFO spreadsheet, change the number of units sold for each purchase so that the value of the inventory by the average cost method and the LIFO method are the same. (Note: you cannot sell more units than were purchased.) Print out a copy of this spreadsheet.

5. If there are 40 units remaining in the ending inventory (7 units from the beginning inventory, 3 units from July 7, 6 units from July 21, 10 units from August 4, 10 units from August 18 and 4 units from August 30) what is the cost of goods sold using the specific identification, average cost, FIFO, and LIFO methods?

6. With the worksheet values from Question 5, change the August 18 cost per unit to $3.05 and the August 30 cost per unit to $3.20. (Be sure to change these values on both spreadsheets.) Which inventory method places the greatest value on the inventory? Which method places the lowest value on the inventory?

7. With the same worksheet values from Question 6, change the number of units purchased on August 18 and August 30 to 15. Now which method places the highest value on the inventory? Which method places the lowest value on the inventory?

8. Reset the original template values using the sample computer screens from the beginning of this project. Record the average cost per unit, the number of units remaining in inventory, and the value of the inventory using the average cost method on paper. Double the number of units purchased for each purchase date, and double the number of units remaining in inventory. What is the change in the average cost per unit? What is the change in the value of the inventory using the average cost method?

9. Using the spreadsheet values from Question 8, increase the cost per unit 20% for each purchase. What is the percent increase in the cost of goods sold using the average cost method? The FIFO method? The LIFO method?

10. Review Question 6. Why did the method with the highest inventory value have that value?

11. Review Question 7. Why did the method with the lowest inventory value have that value?

12. If the cost per unit increases with each purchase, which inventory valuation method should be used if you want the cost of goods sold to be as *low* as possible? Why?

PROJECT 11 ANSWERS

NAME_____   CLASS_____   HOUR_____

1. Specific identification value_____   Cost of goods sold_____

2. Average cost value_____   Cost of goods sold_____

   FIFO value_____   Cost of goods sold_____

   LIFO value_____   Cost of goods sold_____

3. _____

   _____

4. Attach the hard copy to this page.

5. Average cost, cost of goods sold_____

   FIFO, cost of goods sold_____   LIFO, cost of goods sold_____

   Specific identification, cost of goods sold_____

6. Greatest:_____   Lowest:_____

7. Greatest:_____   Lowest:_____

8. Value of the inventory =_____   Average cost_____

9. Average cost_____   FIFO_____   LIFO_____

10. _____

11. _____

12. _____

MATHEMATICS USED IN PROJECT 11

Placing a value on items in inventory is important for various tax documents as well as several of the financial statements used to determine the general health of a business. This project illustrates four of the most commonly accepted methods for placing a value on those goods that are available for sale and on those goods that have been sold. The cost of goods sold figure is useful in determining the profitability of the business.

SPECIFIC IDENTIFICATION

This method of inventory valuation requires the business to know exactly how many units remain in inventory from each purchase the business has made. The value of the inventory can then be calculated by multiplying the cost per unit for the specific purchase by the number of units remaining in inventory from that purchase and then finding the sum of these individual values:

$$\begin{pmatrix} \text{Value of Inventory} \\ \text{for purchase} \end{pmatrix} = \begin{pmatrix} \text{\# of units} \\ \text{on hand} \end{pmatrix} \times \begin{pmatrix} \text{Exact cost} \\ \text{per unit} \end{pmatrix}$$

AVERAGE COST

Under this method of inventory valuation, the cost per unit of the inventory is approximated by calculating the weighted average cost per unit from the purchase record. The weighted average cost per unit is simply the total cost of the units received divided by the total number of units received. Then a value is placed on the remaining inventory by multiplying the number of units on hand by the average cost per unit:

$$\begin{pmatrix} \text{Value of} \\ \text{Inventory} \end{pmatrix} = \begin{pmatrix} \text{\# of units} \\ \text{on hand} \end{pmatrix} \times \begin{pmatrix} \text{Average cost} \\ \text{per unit} \end{pmatrix}$$

FIFO, (FIRST IN FIRST OUT) and LIFO, (LAST IN FIRST OUT)

These methods of inventory valuation assume, regardless of whether it is true or not, that the oldest goods (FIFO) or newest goods (LIFO) are the goods which have been sold. Thus the units remaining in inventory are assumed to be from the most recent (FIFO) or oldest (LIFO) purchases. The units on hand are assigned the per unit cost of the most recent/oldest purchase, up to the total units purchased at that time. If there are more units in the ending inventory than there are in the most recent (FIFO) or oldest (LIFO) purchase then the per unit cost of the next most recent (FIFO) or next oldest (LIFO) purchase is assigned to the remaining number of units on hand up to the total number of units in that purchase and so on until all of the remaining inventory has been assigned a per unit cost. The value of the inventory is computed by multiplying the cost per unit by the number of units assigned to that per unit cost.

For example, using the FIFO method, if 30 units remain in the ending inventory and there were 12 units at $2.00 per unit in the most recent purchase and 20 units at $1.75 in the next most recent purchase, we would assign the per unit cost of $2.00 to 12 of the remaining units and $1.75 to the remaining 18 units on hand, $(30 - 12 = 18)$.

$$\begin{pmatrix} \text{Value of} \\ \text{Inventory} \end{pmatrix} = \begin{pmatrix} \text{\# of units} \\ \text{assigned} \end{pmatrix} \times \begin{pmatrix} \text{Assigned cost} \\ \text{per unit} \end{pmatrix}$$

COST OF GOODS SOLD

The cost of goods sold (COGS) is computed by subtracting the value of the ending inventory from the total cost of the inventory. This assigns a value to the units that have been sold and is useful in measuring the profitability of a business. Cost of goods sold is calculated the same way regardless of the method used to assign a value to the items remaining in inventory.

PROJECT 12
PROPERTY TAX

Sample Computer Screen

Project 12: Property Tax Template

Enter your name in the box to the right   Name: [   ]

Sample Home

Market Value	Assessment Rate	Assessed Value
$120,000.00	35	$42,000.00

Tax Rate in Mills	Annual Property Tax
29	$1,218.00

Total Community Tax Base

Total Market Value	Assessment Rate	Total Assessed Value
$160,000,000.00	35	$56,000,000.00

Tax Rate in Mills	Annual Property Tax
29	$1,624,000.00

DIRECTIONS:

1. Please read all directions. Study and analyze the computer screen before you start answering the questions. Most questions will require information from the computer screens.

2. Open Project 12 by selecting Project_12 on your hard drive or floppy disk (In Excel use File, Open). Set the *zoom* percentage for your screen resolution. For 640 by 480 pixels use a *zoom* setting of 55%, for a screen resolution of 800 by 600 pixels use a *zoom* setting of 75%, and for a screen resolution of 1024 by 768 pixels or higher use a *zoom* setting of 100%.

3. Project 12 contains one spreadsheet.

4. When you enter numeric data, do not include the $ or the , in the number. For example, to enter $1,765.56 you should enter 1765.56. Enter percentages in their decimal form. Only cell values in blue can be changed.

5. If you need to reset the data to the original values for Project 12—as in the sample screens above—simply **reopen the project** by clicking on the Excel commands File, Open and then select Project_12 followed by clicking on yes.

6. To print a copy of the spreadsheet, select the print icon from the top toolbar.

7. To close this project and continue working in Excel, select the *close* option under the File menu. To exit Excel completely click on the X in the upper right corner of the screen. Do not save your work.

PROJECT 12 QUESTIONS

If you have not already done so, reset the information using the sample screens at the beginning of this project.

1. Find the real estate tax on a home with a market value of $50,000.00 in a community whose assessment rate is 35% and whose tax rate is 20 mills; 30 mills; 35 mills; 40 mills; 50 mills; and 60 mills.

2. Find the tax on a home in a community with an assessment rate of 36% of market value and a tax rate of 35 mills if the home has a market value of $50,000; $70,000; $90,000; $100,000; $125,000; $150,000; and $200,000.

3. What is the tax on a home valued at $70,000 with an assessment rate of 35% and a tax rate of 3.6%; a tax rate of $4.28 per $100; a tax rate of $42.50 per thousand? Print out a copy of this worksheet showing the property tax using this last tax rate.

4. If a community has the total of all real estate valued at $50,000,000.00 and an assessment rate of 35%, how much tax revenue is generated when the tax rate is 40 mills; 45 mills; 60 mills; 20 mills; and 30 mills?

5. If you were on a local school board that has a community tax base of $960 million with an assessment rate of 35%, what approximate tax rate would you need to generate $8.5 million in tax revenue?

6. For a community with a total tax base of $500 million and an assessment rate of 40% of market value and a tax rate of 29 mills, what is the total tax? If the market value increased by $30 million what is the *increase* in total tax?

7. Use the $500 million tax base and assessment rate of 40% from Question 6 above. How much *new tax money* is generated if the tax rate increases from 29 mills to 36 mills; 37 mills; 40 mills; and 45 mills?

8. Suppose your home is located in a community with an assessment rate of 30% of market value and a property tax rate of 45 mills. If the market value of your house was $480,000 last year and is increased to $510,000 this year, what is the increase in your property taxes?

9. Suppose your home is located in a community with an assessment rate of 30% of market value and a property tax rate of 45 mills. If the market value of your house is $185,000 and the community approved an additional 9 mill school levy, what is the increase in your property taxes?

10. Suppose your home is located in a community with an assessment rate of 35% of market value and a property tax rate of 42 mills. If the market value of your house was $250,000 last year and the market value increases 12% this year, what is the increase in your property taxes? Is this a 12% increase in property tax? Explain.

11. Put your cursor in cell E7 and record the contents of the cell. Write this "Excel" formula as a typical "math" formula and record it on the answer sheet.

PROJECT 12 ANSWERS

NAME_____   CLASS_____   HOUR_____

1. 20 mills_____   25 mills_____   30 mills_____

    35 mills_____   40 mills_____   50 mills_____

    60 mills_____

2. $50,000_____ $70,000_____ $90,000_____

    $100,000_____ $125,000_____ $150,000_____

    $200,000_____

3. 3.6%_____ $4.28 per hundred_____ $42.50 per thousand_____

4. 40 mills_____   45 mills_____   35 mills_____

    20 mills_____   30 mills_____

5. Tax rate_____mills

6. Total tax_____

    Increase in total tax_____

7. 36 mills_____   37_____   40_____   45_____

8. Increase in property tax_____

9. Increase in property tax_____

10. Increase in property tax_____   Percent change in taxes_____

    _____

11. _____   _____

71

MATHEMATICS USED IN PROJECT 12

Property tax calculations make extensive use of the basic percent equation, $P = B \times R$. In calculating the assessed value of a home, the base is the home's market value and the rate is the community's assessment rate. The part we would calculate then is the home's assessed value. The same holds true when we consider the total community tax base. The base is the total market value of property in the community, the rate is the community assessment rate, and the calculated part is the total assessed value of the property in the community.

> **Example::** A home with a market value of $165,000 resides in a
> community with an assessment rate of 30% of the market
> value. The assessed value of the home then would be;
> Assessed Value = Assessment Rate × Market Value and so,
> Assessed Value = $0.30 \times \$165,000 = \$49,500$

Tax rates in this project *must* be expressed in *mills*; thus, if you are given a tax rate in dollars per $100 of assessed value or dollars per $1,000 of assessed value or in percent form you must convert the rate to mills. To complete these conversions you may use the formulas below.

To convert a tax rate in dollars per $100 of assessed value to mills:

Mills = tax rate (dollars per $100 of assessed value) times 10.

Example: A tax rate of $3.50 per $100 $= 3.5 \times 10$ mills $= 35$ mills

To convert a tax rate in percent form to mills:

Mills = tax rate (in percent form) times 10.

Example: A tax rate of 3.5% $= 3.5 \times 10$ mills $= 35$ mills

To convert a tax rate in dollars per $1000 of assessed value to mills:

Mills = tax rate (dollars per $1000 of assessed value). They are numerically equal.

Example: A tax rate of $35.00 per $1000 $= 35$ mills.

PROJECT 13
DESCRIPTIVE STATISTICS

Sample Computer Screens

Project 13: Descriptive Statistics Templates

INDIVIDUAL DATA

Enter your name in the box to the right   Name: [   ]

Data Table

40	42	45	43	44	45	45
50	38	38	38	38	25	16
12	24	26	21	15	18	42
6	50	10	13	12	12	18
34	33	25	42	12	18	25
36	18	44	35	18	22	24

Descriptive Statistics

Mean	28.86	Maximum	50
Median	25.5	Minimum	6
Mode	18	Range	44

Project 13: Descriptive Statistics Templates

GROUPED DATA

Enter your name in the box to the right   Name: [   ]

Data Intervals			Midpoint of Interval	Frequency (number of data values in interval)	Midpoint x Frequency
90	to	99	94.5	5	472.5
80	to	89	84.5	8	676
70	to	79	74.5	12	894
60	to	69	64.5	6	387
50	to	59	54.5	2	109
40	to	49	44.5	0	0
30	to	39	34.5	1	34.5
20	to	29	24.5	0	0
10	to	19	14.5	0	0
0	to	9	4.5	0	0

Total number of data values	34

Mean	75.68

73

Project 13: Descriptive Statistics Templates

Enter your name in the box to the right

Name: [   ]

Data Set I: Sales

Month	Sales (thousands)
Jan	145
Feb	150
Mar	160
Apr	120
May	95
Jun	90
Jul	100
Aug	110
Sep	95
Oct	120
Nov	145
Dec	180

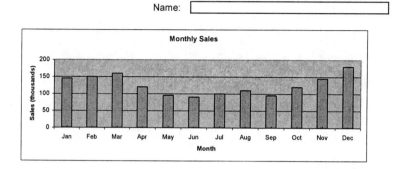

Scroll Down for Next Graph

Data Set II: Monthly Budget

Item	Expense
Salaries	$128,000
Overtime	$32,000
Insurance	$18,000
Utilities	$25,000
Materials	$5,000
Taxes	$12,000
Misc.	$45,000

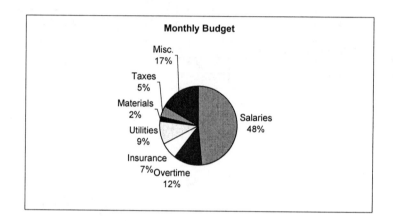

Scroll Down for Next Graph

Data Set III: Student Enrollment Each Quarter by Gender

Quarter	Men	Women
Autumn	3250	4110
Winter	3020	4300
Spring	2750	2550
Summer	1240	1020

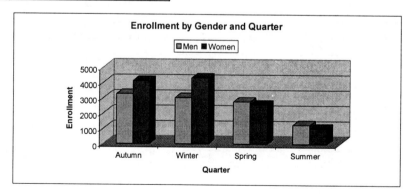

DIRECTIONS:

1. Please read all directions. Study and analyze the computer screens before you start answering the questions. Most questions will require information from the computer screens.

2. Open Project 13 by selecting Project_13 on your hard drive or floppy disk (In Excel use File, Open). Set the *zoom* percentage for your screen resolution. For 640 by 480 pixels use a *zoom* setting of 55%, for a screen resolution of 800 by 600 pixels use a *zoom* setting of 75%, and for a screen resolution of 1024 by 768 pixels or higher use a *zoom* setting of 100%.

3. Project 13 contains three spreadsheets: Descriptive Stats Raw Data, Descriptive Stats Grouped Data, and Graphics. Use the tabs at the bottom of the screen to move among the spreadsheets.

4. When you enter numeric data, do not include the $ or the , in the number. For example, to enter $1,765.56 you should enter 1765.56. Only cell values in blue can be changed.

5. If you need to reset the data to the original values for Project 13—as in the sample screens above—simply **reopen the project** by clicking on the Excel commands File, Open and then select Project_13 followed by clicking on yes.

6. To print a copy of the spreadsheet, select the print icon from the top toolbar. Printing the graphics spreadsheet is not recommended.

7. To close this project and continue working in Excel, select the *close* option under the File menu. To exit Excel completely click on the X in the upper right corner of the screen. Do not save your work.

PROJECT 13 QUESTIONS

If you have not already done so, reset the information using the sample screens at the beginning of this project.

1. On the Descriptive Stats Raw Data spreadsheet, enter the data values 45, 6, 78, 12, 34, 43, 89, 56, 32, 34, 55, 44, 33, and 17 in the data table. Delete the values in the remainder of the data table. What are the mean, median, and range of this set of data?

2. Now enter the number 325 in one of the empty data boxes. What are the mean, median, and range of this set of data? Which measure of central tendency, the mean or the median, appears to be more sensitive to extreme values?

3. To the data in the previous exercise, add 23, 45, 67, 21, 45, 67, 78, 45, 67, 34, 56, 89, 76, 45, 34, 23, 89, and 43 by placing these values in data boxes without data values. What are the mean, median, and range of this set of data? How much did the mean change from your answer in Question 2?

4. Delete the data value 325 from the data table in Question 3. Print out a copy of this spreadsheet and count up the number of data values in the 90's, 80's, 70's, etc.

5a. Switch to the Descriptive Stats Grouped Data and enter the same your summary from Question 4 as frequencies for each of the intervals. What is the mean? How does this compare with the mean from the Raw Data spreadsheet?

5b. Why might the answers be different in Questions 4 and 5a?

6. Enter the following data on the Raw Data spreadsheet and as frequencies on the Grouped Data spreadsheet.
    12, 16, 19, 14, 16, 23, 25, 30, 32, 39, 42, 45, 47, 48, 48, 51, 56, 53,
    58, 57, 51, 63, 64, 67, 71, 72, 73, 74, 75, 76, 77, 78, 79, 83, 83, 85,
    86, 89, 81, 83, 88, 91, 99, 93, 96, 95, 96, 98, 98, 91.
    What is the mean from the Raw Data spreadsheet and the Grouped Data spreadsheet? How do these compare?

7. Look at the Graphics spreadsheet. For the first data set, which month had the greatest amount of sales and which month had the least? Can you see any trends in the sales figures? Was it easier to determine this from the graph or from the table of values?

8. On the Graphics spreadsheet, from the pie graph for data set II, which budget item has the greatest cost? What percent of the budget is devoted to this item?

9. Look at data set III on the Graphics spreadsheet. Which quarter has the highest total enrollment? Which quarter has the highest female enrollment?

10. On the Graphics spreadsheet, for data set I, increase the sales amounts for even months, (Feb, Apr, etc.) by 10% and decrease the sales figures for the odd months by 20%, (Jan, Mar, etc.). Now which month had the greatest sales figures and which had the least? Can you see any trends in evident in the graph?

11. Use data set II and your own personal budget items to produce a pie graph of your monthly expenses. Print out a copy of this graph by clicking on the print button on the Excel toolbar. What item do you spend the most amount of money on each month?

12. Using the Grouped Data spreadsheet, put your cursor in cell E9 and record the contents of the cell. Write this "Excel" formula as a typical "math" formula and record it on the answer sheet.

PROJECT 13 ANSWERS

NAME_____   CLASS_____   HOUR_____

1.   Mean_____   Median_____   Range_____

2.   Mean_____   Median_____   Range_____

More sensitive_____

3.   Mean_____   Median_____   Range_____

Change in means_____

4.   90's_____   80's_____   70's_____   60's_____

50's_____   40's_____   30's_____   20's_____

10's_____   1's_____

5a.   Mean_____   Comparison_____

5b.   _____

6.   Raw data mean_____   Grouped data mean_____

Comparison_____

7.   Greatest_____   Least_____   Trends_____

_____

8.   Greatest_____   Percentage of budget_____

9.   Highest enrollment_____   Highest female enrollment_____

10.   Greatest_____   Least_____   Trends_____

_____

11.   _____

Attach your printout of the pie graph.

12.   _____   _____

MATHEMATICS USED IN PROJECT 13

USING RAW DATA: Descriptive Stats Raw Data Spreadsheet

The mean of n data values is the sum of all n data values divided by n. That is,

$$m = Mean = \frac{x_1 + x_2 + x_3 + \cdots + x_n}{n} \, ,$$

where $x_1, x_2, x_3, \cdots x_n$ represent data value #1, #2, #3, $\cdots$ up to the *nth* (or last) piece of data.

The maximum and minimum data values are the smallest and largest numbers in the data set. These two numbers are used to determine the range of the data. The range is the difference between the maximum data value and the minimum data value. $RANGE = maximum - minimum$. The range is used to measure the amount of variability in the data.

USING GROUPED DATA: Descriptive Stats Grouped Data Spreadsheet

When working with grouped data, each data value in an interval is treated as if it were the midpoint of that interval. So, for example, for the data values 56, 58, and 51, all of which fit into the data interval from 50 to 59, all three numbers are assumed to be 54.5, the midpoint of the data interval. By treating the data in this way, the mean of the data set will be slightly different than if the data is entered individually. If there are many data values however, or the data values in each interval are evenly distributed over the interval, then the error will be small. The mean is the sum of the product of the midpoint and the frequency for each interval divided by the total number of data values represented in the table (the sum of the frequencies).

INTERPRETING GRAPHS: Graphics spreadsheet

The Graphics spreadsheet illustrates three common types of statistical and business graphs. The first is a standard bar graph that compares values for several categories; in this case we are comparing sales by month. The second graph is a pie graph which is very useful in representing how a total quantity, in this case a monthly budget, is distributed over several categories, in this case common budget items. The final graph is a three-dimensional bar graph showing how two categories, male and female enrollments, compare with each other over several different periods, quarters.